ANALYZING INEQUALITY

STUDIES IN SOCIAL INEQUALITY

LIFE CHANCES AND SOCIAL MOBILITY
IN COMPARATIVE PERSPECTIVE

Edited by Stefan Svallfors

STANFORD UNIVERSITY PRESS
STANFORD, CALIFORNIA

Stanford University Press
Stanford, California

ISBN: 978-0-8047--5757-7

ISBN: 978-0-8047-5096-7

Library of Congress Cataloging-in-Publication Data
    Analyzing inequality : life chances and social
mobility in comparative perspective / edited by
Stefan Svallfors.
        p.   cm.
    Conference proceedings.
    Includes bibliographical references and index.

    1. Equality.   2. Social mobility.   I. Svallfors,
Stefan.

HM821.A53   2005
305.5 — dc22
                                2005003181

Original Printing 2005

Last figure below indicates year of this printing:
14   13   12   11   10   09   08   07

Typeset by G & S Typesetters, Inc. in 10/14 Sabon

FOR ROBERT ERIKSON

CONTENTS

Tables

Figures

CONTRIBUTORS

Stefan Svallfors is professor of sociology at Umeå University, Sweden. His research deals mainly with the comparative study of attitudes and values and their links to social structure and institutions. His current research focuses on class differences in attitudes in Sweden, Britain, Germany, and the United States.

Sara Arber is head of the school of human sciences at the University of Surrey, where she was promoted to a personal Chair in 1994. She is codirector of the Centre for Research on Ageing and Gender (CRAG). Professor Arber's research focuses on gender and class inequalities in health and on aging and later life.

Tony Atkinson is the warden, Nuffield College, Oxford University. Sir Tony Atkinson's major research field is public economics, and his current research topics are economics of income distribution and poverty and microeconomics. He also has been working on the distribution of income, on the interrelation between social policy and the macroeconomy, and on the economics of poverty, social exclusion, and the welfare state.

John Goldthorpe is Emeritus Fellow of Nuffield College, Oxford University. Dr. Goldthorpe's intellectual interests lie in social stratification and mobility, sociological theory, sociological methodology, and the relationship between theory and research. He is one of the leading figures in the analysis of social classes and mobility.

Karl Ulrich Mayer is professor of sociology at Yale University and director at the Max Planck Institute for Human Development in Berlin. Karl Ulrich Mayer has done empirical quantitative research on, among else, images of society, intergenerational social mobility, vocational training, higher education, job shifts and career mobility, labor market segmentation, women's employment, and family demography.

Annemette Sørensen is a sociologist specializing in the study of gender stratification in North America and Europe. She is a lecturer at the department of sociology at Harvard University. Her current research is a comparative study of economic inequality between men and women in Europe and the United States toward the end of the 20th century.

PREFACE

The chapters in this volume developed from papers presented at a symposium to honor Robert Erikson, on his retirement as Secretary General for the Swedish Council for Working Life and Social Research. The symposium was held at Sigtunahöjden, outside Stockholm, November 24–25, 2003. The contributors to the volume would like to extend their collective thanks to the council, and in particular its administrative director Erland Bergman, for hosting the conference.

We also want to thank the commentators on the papers who contributed to making the symposium a true intellectual feast and to improving the quality of the volume. In order of appearance: Gunn Elisabeth Birkelund, Walter Korpi, Johan Fritzell, Inga Persson, Janne Jonsson, Denny Vågerö, Elianne Riska, Ulla Björnberg, Eva Bernhardt, Rune Åberg, and Anders Björklund. A special thanks is due to Richard Breen for presenting John Goldthorpe's paper in place of the author.

While standing on their own feet, the papers brought together in this volume also reflect the substantive research fields of Robert Erikson's distinguished career, through their focus on social mobility and life chances in comparative perspective. We can only hope they also reflect Robert's intellectual style in summarizing results from theoretically guided rigorous empirical research in an accessible and yet nontrivial form. The authors of the chapters included here have all, in one way or another, enjoyed the good fortune of having worked with Robert, and the dedication of this volume to him is but a small repayment of the intellectual debt we owe.

Stefan Svallfors, Umeå, September 2004

ANALYZING INEQUALITY

CHAPTER ONE

Introduction

Stefan Svallfors

The study of inequality is an intrinsic aspect of modern social science. Issues concerning the distribution of life chances, incomes, mobility and opportunity, poverty, and social exclusion have had a prominent place in the social sciences since their inception. In all likelihood, these issues will remain on the social scientific agenda indefinitely. This book aims to take stock of what has been achieved in selected subfields within the larger field of inequality studies. By summarizing the state of the art in topics such as life courses, social mobility, and the comparative use of social indicators and family effects on stratification, we hope to show both that the analysis of inequality has tackled and answered an array of important sociological questions, and that important tasks lie ahead.

The study of inequality fuses normative, descriptive, and explanatory aspects in a way that links the field both to public policy and social theory. As descriptions, studies of inequality explore *how much* inequality there is in quantitative terms: who gets what compared to others? The explanatory analysis tries to find out *why* some get more than others: which social processes at the micro- and macro-levels lie behind the outcome patterns social scientists observe? The normative analysis of inequality is a more philosophical pursuit and asks whether the current state of inequality can be regarded as *just*: by what standards is the distribution of various goods and burdens to be considered fair or unfair, and to whom? These three aspects of the analysis of inequality are interlinked, but they have an asymmetrical relationship. It is perfectly possible to have a description of the current level of inequality without ever raising the question about why it came into existence, or whether it is fair or unfair. But in order to explain differences and changes in inequality, accurate descriptions are crucial; and in order to decide whether inequality is just or unjust, information is needed both about the amount of inequality and why it has come to be.

The chapters compiled in this volume all, in different ways, take stock of the current situation in the analysis of inequality. In doing so, the authors demonstrate that the analysis of inequality has reached new levels of sophistication over the course of the last few decades. Progress is clearly visible both in the quality of data, in the application of methods, and in the kind of theoretical explanations that the authors put forward.

Regarding *data*, three kinds of databases created over the last couple of decades are especially important in the analysis of inequality. The first is truly a longitudinal database, where the same set of individuals is followed over an extended period of time. Such data are immensely valuable because they allow the problem of causality to be tackled more successfully than can be achieved by using cross-sectional data. A perennial problem in analyzing inequality (or any other social process) is that of distinguishing between causality and selection (Ni Bhrolcháin 2001). In contrast to cross-sectional data, panel data will, if properly analyzed, allow the establishment of the time order of events and therefore makes it possible for the analyst to distinguish between causal and selection effects.

A particularly efficient form of longitudinal databases allows register data on various social outcomes (incomes, births, marriages, mortality, etc.) to be merged with survey data on current and past experiences. Examples of two particularly rich datasets in this respect are the two variants of level-of-living surveys conducted in Sweden, by the Swedish Institute for Social Research [www.sofi.su.se/LNU2000/english.htm] and by Statistics Sweden [www.scb.se/templates/Product____12199.asp (all information at this web page is in Swedish)].

The second type of data is derived from cross-national comparative databases. By using such data, analysts may be able to study the impact of national institutions on levels and processes of inequality. A large amount of work has been put into creating truly comparative databases, a challenging task given the difficulties of finding equivalent indicators and harmonizing national official statistics. Two of the most valuable datasets currently available illustrate different approaches to tackling these problems. The Luxembourg Income Study (LIS), the adjoined Luxembourg Employment Study (LES), and the new Luxembourg Wealth Study (LWS) [www.lisproject.org]

depend on post-harmonization of data from national surveys (household income surveys and labor force surveys). In contrast, the new European Social Survey (ESS) [www.europeansocialsurvey.org] tries to construct comparability in the original indicators before the surveys are fielded, through an elaborate procedure for securing cross-national validity of samples, indicators, and translations.

The ESS is also an example of a third type of database, one in which objective and subjective data are integrated. The most longstanding such survey is the International Social Survey Program (ISSP, www.issp.org). The ISSP has conducted several modules on "Social Inequality" (1987, 1992, and 1999), and the modules on "The Role of Government" (1985, 1990, 1996, and 2006) also contain data of relevance for the study of inequality. The ESS has been conducted two times, in 2002 and 2004, and will continue as a biannual survey. It contains several attitudinal subthemes of relevance for the topic of inequality, in addition to encompassing data concerning actual resources and living conditions.

The importance of surveys such as the ISSP and ESS lies in the possibility to link subjective aspects of inequality (identities, aspirations, norms, etc.) with measures of actual positions in the stratification system. Such subjective indicators may be seen both as an *outcome* of the stratification process, and as something *affecting* processes of inequality. For example, support for redistribution of market outcomes are to a large degree the effect of the actual experiences of stratification effects (Svallfors 2004). Such support may in turn, if channeled into political support for parties set on building redistributive institutions, affect future stratification patterns and outcomes.

While the situation regarding data in many respects looks bright, two unfortunate circumstances should be pointed out. One is that the particularly rich data that is now compiled by the European Union, data that national statistical agencies are required to collect in each union country, are expensive and difficult to use for the research community. These data are to a large extent harmonized already at the point of collection, which makes them exceptionally valuable for comparative research on inequality processes and outcomes. The use of these data in the research community has however been hampered by (1) the long time lag in the release of the statistics, (2) the extreme data protection measures applied, and (3) the sometimes prohibitively expensive charges for users.

A second problem in data access and comparability is what seems to be a lack of coordination and cooperation between EU-Europe and the United States. The new European Social Survey has no counterpart in the United States; the European Union data, of course, has no counterpart in the United States either. A new European Cohort Study is in its planning stages, apparently with no intended cooperation across the Atlantic [www.fas.forskning.se/en/newsletter/2003/nl103.pdf]. Because the European model of capitalism, in all its variants, is substantially different from the American one, it is highly unfortunate that available data allow only limited comparisons between Europe and the United States. As several of the contributors to this volume point out, the institutional differences between Europe and the United States are likely to be reflected in substantial differences in levels and processes of inequality, but such arguments can now often be exposed to only limited and indirect tests.

The progress in terms of data access has been matched by innovations and new directions in the *methods* applied to such data. Three important improvements should be mentioned. The first is the invention and dissemination of techniques for analyzing longitudinal data (for an introduction, see Blossfeld and Rohwer 2002). Because such data as pointed out above are particularly valuable in trying to establish causal links, it is very useful to be in possession of statistical techniques that allow these data to be successfully analyzed.

A second major improvement is the proliferation of techniques for analyzing categorical data (for an introduction, see Long 1997). Because many of the inequality outcomes of interest are categorical (either a person goes on to university or not; either a person becomes unemployed or not) and not linear, standard regression techniques are often unsuited to the questions analysts want to answer. In such cases, a variety of nonlinear regression techniques are now available alongside other techniques such as loglinear modeling and latent class analysis.

A third valuable improvement in the array of analytical techniques is the increasing use of multilevel analysis (for an introduction, see Hox 2002). Many of the most important causes behind inequality are not tied to individuals but are properties of the contexts in which these individuals are embedded. Information about this context is often crucial for understanding stratification processes. Because such data have a nested structure (for example, an individual can be placed in a certain classroom situation, which in turn is embedded in a local community, which in turn is part of a national policy regime), standard statistical techniques are inappropriate and can yield invalid results.

The basics of all these statistical innovations have been known for a long time, in many cases several decades, and have been widely used for some time. Their application in routine analytical use requires that appropriate easy-to-use software is available, in order to make investment costs less prohibitive. The past couple of decades have seen considerable improvements in this regard.

The list of improvements hitherto provided may strike readers as unduly technical in its emphasis on data access and statistical techniques. Nevertheless, progress in the field is clearly visible also when it comes to *theory and explanations*. Such progress is highly dependent on the improvements in data and statistical techniques but also relies on new thinking, occurring at the boundaries between sociology, economics, and political science.

One such important development, at the boundaries between sociology and political science, is the increasing focus on institutions in effecting distributive outcomes. The concept "institution" is notoriously slippery, but according to one workable definition institutions are "the rules of the game" (North 1990: 3–5), or to use a stricter definition "the formal rules, compliance procedures, and standard operating practices that structure the relationship between individuals in various units of the polity and economy" (Hall 1992: 96; cf. Levi 1990: 405). This definition of institutions only includes deliberately designed objects, such as social security systems, political party systems, collective bargaining systems, and so on, while leaving social facts such as family interactions, class structures, and norms outside the definition. Even based on this fairly narrow definition, it is clear that the presence and impact of institutions are immense in modern societies.

Institutions impinge on distributive processes and outcomes in a number of ways. They modify the structure of rewards and costs inherent in employment contracts, through welfare state intervention or labor market legislation, for example. This modification may either be achieved directly, through keeping employment contracts within certain legal limits, or indirectly through welfare state benefits and taxes or by subsidizing the consumption of goods such as health care and education. Institutions also structure possibilities and incentives. Political institutions structure competition, recruitment, and social mobility, therefore affecting the incentives of social actors.

Important aspects of distributive processes, such as wage setting (Pontusson et al. 2002), income distribution (Korpi and Palme 1998), or access to the labor market (Daly and Rake 2003) are structured by institutions of various kinds. Institutions introduce an element of historical contingency into the play of market forces, modifying market outcomes or even affecting access to the market.

To focus on institutions is therefore to analyze how macro factors impinge on micro action in the creation and maintenance of inequality. Some important strands of current thinking about inequality focus inversely on the micro foundations for macro outcomes. These lines of theorizing occur mainly at the boundaries between sociology and economics. The aim is to model how purposeful action can explain macro social outcomes (such as the distribution of opportunity or resources). Two—partly competing and partly complementary—variants seem to be particularly important. The first focuses on the networks in which people find themselves embedded (Tilly 1998; White 1992; Granovetter 1995). In this rendition, inequality results from the transmission of resources and constraints through networks, as exemplified by migration chains, network recruitment, and diffusion processes, and from inclusion in or exclusion from such networks.

The second version focuses on individual choice within constraints (Goldthorpe 2000, in particular chs. 5, 6, 8, 9). Here we find a focus on rational action, in which individual's (subjective) rationality is the guiding principle behind courses taken. Inequalities in outcomes should be seen here as resulting from the very different constraints facing actors in different positions, rather than in their differing cognitive or emotional evaluation of the choices themselves. A prime example is found in the efforts to explain differing propensities to seek higher education in different social classes, even at constant levels of school grades. The rational action framework here tends to emphasize the different constraints facing children from different class backgrounds rather than class differences in "cultural resistance" against higher education as such (Goldthorpe 2000: chs. 8–9; Erikson and Jonsson 1996).

The developments regarding data, methods, and theory/explanations are mutually dependent. Without new questions about the impact of institutions on inequality, little impetus is provided for the cumbersome process of collecting cross-national comparative data. Without new techniques for analyzing data, these data will remain underutilized and unable to answer the questions put by theoretical developments. Without access to appropriate data and analytical techniques, theory and explanation turn into mere conceptualization or armchair guesswork. If the field of inequality analyses is to continue to thrive, it will depend on a continuous and concerted development of data, statistical techniques, and theory/explanations.

The chapters that follow both draw on and illustrate the current state of research. In Chapter Two, Karl Ulrich Mayer paints the history and current state of comparative life course research. In the first part of his chapter, he tells the story of how life course research developed from a highly general and universal account of stages of human development into a differential life course sociology.

Mayer then follows the attempts to map historical variation in the analysis of life courses. These attempts soon run into severe problems of linking historical periodization with specific patterns of life course outcomes. Historical periodization and the lifetimes of individuals are not coordinated, which make any causal inferences hazardous and uncertain.

Mayer argues that cross-national comparison is a way out, and that it offers a particularly fruitful strategy if researchers want to untangle the complex relationships between institutional characteristics and life course outcomes. Such comparisons may take different directions. A particularly influential direction argues that institutions tend to appear in bundles, conceptualized as "regimes" or "varieties of capitalism." Mayer argues that even though these attempts took social scientists a long way in the establishment of causal relations between institutional arrangements and life course, problems appeared also in this vein of research. The problem is that cross-national institutional variation, and the effects on life course outcomes, defy neat and easy categorization into regimes or varieties of capitalism. The links between institutional setups and individuals' life courses become blurred by such an "over-aggregation" of institutional variation.

Therefore, Mayer maintains that the most feasible way forward is country-specific comparative analysis. Only in this way will it be possible to establish the causal links between institutional macro factors and life course patterns and outcomes. In order to show how such linkages may be established, Mayer turns next to a comparative analysis of institutions and life courses in the United States, Germany, and Sweden. He shows how institutional differences among the three countries in schooling systems, production and firm organization, welfare policies, and labor market relations and regulations tend to give widely differing outcomes in life course outcomes and transitions. From leaving the nest, family formation, transition from school to work, work-life mobility, to poverty rates and durations, the institutional arrangements in each country affect most aspects of life courses in one way or another.

Mayer concludes his chapter by arguing that a focus on country specificity does not necessarily lead to a multitude of unrelated studies and unwieldy variation. If a clear focus is maintained on the mechanisms through which institutions exert their influence, systematic patterns of association are detected beneath the specificity of national arrangements.

In Chapter Three, John Goldthorpe asks whether anything that can be described as "progress" might be discerned within sociology. Goldthorpe points out that sociologists have often tended to answer the question in the negative. Such writers argue either that progress is in principle impossible in social science because all knowledge is context-bound to such an extent that any attempt at generalization becomes impossible, or that although intellectual progress would be possible in the social sciences, none can be observed within sociology.

Goldthorpe argues that both accounts are mistaken. Rather than engaging in a theoretical or philosophical argument about the case, he goes about showing that progress *has* actually occurred within at least one particular subfield within sociology, that of social mobility research. According to Goldthorpe, cumulative knowledge growth may actually be observed within social mobility research to an extent that it belies any argument about the impossibility or nonoccurrence of progress in sociology.

Goldthorpe summarizes progress within social mobility research under four headings: data, concepts and analysis, empirical findings, and theory. Regarding data, the improvements are obvious in terms of both coverage and quality. Coverage has been improved through the growth and routine replication of general-purpose surveys through which data of a repeated cross-sectional kind now allow comparisons both across nations and through time. Quality has improved regarding consistent codings of occupational and educational data, again both across and within countries.

Regarding concepts and analysis, Goldthorpe emphasizes that social scientists should not expect progress to take the form of the gradual movement toward "one best way." He rather points to progress in terms of how specific conceptual problems have been tackled and solved. One particularly important advance in this respect was when mobility research managed to get out of the impasse in which it found itself when trying to apply the concepts of "structural" versus "exchange" mobility. The introduction of loglinear modeling allowed the problem to be reformulated as the more viable and revealing distinction between "absolute" and "relative" mobility rates.

The empirical findings may be summarized as a series of empirical regularities that have been established across a relatively wide range of institutional and cultural contexts. One such important finding is that endogenous mobility regimes, measured as patterns of relative mobility rates, show both a high degree of temporal stability and a fundamental similarity across nations. Accordingly, the documentation of change and variation in absolute mobility rates has to be attributed mainly to changes and differences in the occupational structure within and across countries.

A second important finding is that although the most important factor mediating intergenerational mobility is educational attainment, direct effects from class origin on destination class nevertheless persist. Furthermore, no steady increase of the importance of education may be detected, as would have been predicted by many theories about change in industrial society.

That last observation leads Goldthorpe to conclude that functionalist theories, which would predict increasingly open and meritocratic societies, by and large fail to make sense of the empirical findings from mobility research. Goldthorpe argues that a more micro-oriented theory of rational action has been more successful in explaining mobility outcomes, and that in important respects these kinds of theories are already used to model the relationship between, for example, class background and educational achievement.

In sum, Goldthorpe maintains that considerable progress has been made within social mobility research and the question then arises as to why such progress is such a rare event in sociology. Why has mobility research made progress while many other sociological research fields have not? Goldthorpe emphasizes that because research is a collective product, the explanation should be sought in the way social mobility researchers have chosen to organize. In particular, the wide-ranging institutionalization of international exchange and collaboration, as expressed foremost in the Research Committee on Social Stratification and Mobility (RC28), has been important. In Goldthorpe's view, this international profile has helped social mobility researchers to stick to fairly well-defined and "doable" problems in a sustained manner; it has also helped to protect the research field from "the distractions of ideology and fashion." The question of why other research fields have *not* been organized in a similar manner remains to be answered.

Chapter Four, by Tony Atkinson, illustrates the close connection between the analysis of inequality and public policies, by focusing on the use of social indicators in research and policy. The use of social indicators is an attempt to directly measure social problems and levels of living, instead of relying on indirect measures such as income. Both the European Union and the United Nations have agreed on a number of social indicators to be used as a baseline against which to evaluate policy effects and social change.

Atkinson argues that from a policy point of view, the increasing use of social indicators has been fairly successful by raising awareness of the extent of social problems and by emphasizing political responsibility for solving them. However, the success has only been qualified, due both to problematic links between indicators and policy design, and to conceptualization and measurement problems in the social indicators themselves.

Atkinson particularly points to three of these unsolved problems. One is the conflation of inputs and outputs. For example, it is unclear whether income distribution should be considered an output measure, as often is the case, or if it should not rather be seen as an input measure, because it is just an intermediate vehicle in achieving a fair distribution of well-being. It is important to keep measures of effort separate from measures of end results, and that has not always been the case in comparative analyses.

A second problematic feature is the rush to aggregate indicators into summary measures of well-being. Atkinson points out that such aggregation is highly problematic. For example, it is not clear whether aggregation should take place through aggregating indicators, or though summing individuals with different combinations of deprivation. Furthermore, and perhaps even more problematic, there exists no standard according to which such a summary measure should be constructed. What weights should be attached to different components of a summary measure? What is the yardstick against which different components should be measured?

A third problem that Atkinson points to is the ambivalence regarding nationality; that is, the question of whether success is measured simply by the number of people above a certain threshold, or whether researchers care about distributions within individual countries. A fourfold increase in the rate of poverty in Sweden, for example, would be a dramatic change for that country but would hardly make any difference on a world or even European scale. Conversely, a minor change around the poverty line in China would lift tens of millions of people from poverty and make a substantial impact on the world level.

Atkinson further points out that linking indicators to policies is highly problematic. The main issue is that if changes in the chosen indicators are taken as the sole yardstick against which to evaluate policy, or even for targeting support to developing countries, this measurement may create too strong of incentives to concentrate on these particular goals at the expense of others. Atkinson makes the observation that this process has an uncanny similarity to the production targets set by Soviet-type economies and that similar social inefficiencies are likely to follow.

The last problem Atkinson deals with is measuring levels versus measuring change. He argues that these processes are really two different things and require use of different indicators for measuring levels and for measuring change. For example, in measuring global poverty it may be advisable to use a purchasing power adjustment to establish the base poverty line, but measuring change requires applying national price changes in each country. These measurements may then increase the risk that findings from comparing levels and comparing change may yield inconsistent results.

In sum, Atkinson concludes that the increased use of social indicators has been beneficial in many ways, but that important problems need to be solved if the full potential of social indicators research is to be fulfilled.

One important factor affecting the structure of inequality is the decreasing stability in family relationships over the last few decades. In Chapter Five, Annemette Sørensen asks what have been the effects of this development for social inequality. Sørensen argues that the family plays an important part in the stratification system for three reasons. First, it is a redistributive unit in which resources are pooled and shared. Second, the family serves as source of constraints and encouragements for the achievements of its individual members. Third, it is an important source for the intergenerational maintenance of inequality.

Sørensen wants to discuss what the effects on inequality have been of changes in the family composition and stability over the last decades. The findings come from the United States, where most of the relevant research has been done. The United States could be seen as something of a "worst case scenario," because other risk-hedging and redistributive institutions apart from the family are so weak.

Sørensen first asks to what extent increase in family and household inequality can be attributed to changes in family structure and women's earnings. She finds that the increase in the number of single mother households as well as the growth in single-person households has been one of the sources for increasing inequality in the United States. It is considerably less clear whether the increase in women's earnings has played any large part, although all studies show that increasing inequality in men's earnings has had an important impact.

Second, Sørensen asks whether greater inequality among children has resulted from the changes in family structure. Here, different pieces of research point in different directions, but overall, it seems that changes in family structure have created more inequality in children's attainment than would have been the case if these changes had not taken place. Such differences in educational achievement are then likely to be transferred to increasing inequality in occupational attainment and earnings.

Third, Sørensen asks if the family's ability to transmit advantage to their children has been weakened or, to put it differently, whether the mobility regime has become more fluid as a result of changes in the family. Less family stability could be expected to lead to less close links between family background and individual achievement. On balance, this conclusion is also what Sørensen finds in the literature. Association between origins and destinations is weaker for all "alternative" family forms than they are for two-parent intact families. This finding suggests that as fewer children grow up in two-parent families social scientists may expect intergenerational mobility patterns to become more fluid.

In conclusion, Sørensen discusses to what extent the findings from the United States can be applied to other countries. Sørensen argues that on the one hand, the welfare state in the United States offers a particularly weak buffer against downward mobility and poverty connected to divorce and single motherhood. In more encompassing welfare states, the detrimental effects of marriage dissolution are likely to be weaker. On the other hand, in no country is it likely that the effects of growing family instability will be completely mitigated by welfare policies.

One important aspect of contemporary analyses of inequality has been an increased emphasis on changes over the life cycle and their connections to the institutional framework. In Chapter Six, Sara Arber illustrates this by arguing for the importance of taking gender and family status into account when analyzing inequalities in later life. Arber notes that less attention has been paid to inequalities in later life than might had been expected, given that the period spent after retirement is becoming almost as long as the time spent in employment. Alternative theoretical frameworks for understanding inequality in later life have been formulated. Some of these frameworks argue that inequalities in later life tend to become attenuated, although others point to continuity from working life, or even increasing inequalities between groups in later life. The research hitherto conducted has, however, focussed mostly on class at the expense of gender and family status. In addition, although some research has been conducted on older women, older men have rarely been the object of research.

Using data from Britain, Arber sets out to correct some of these shortcomings. She focuses on how gender and family status affect material circumstances and social relations, and health-related behavior such as smoking and drinking alcohol.

Several interesting results emerge from Arber's analysis. Widows are likely to be materially disadvantaged compared to married women, but their patterns of social relations (as measured by contacts with relatives, friends, and neighbors) are similar to married women. In contrast, widowers differ little from married men in their material resources, but they have significantly fewer social contacts. A drastic summary would be to say that widows become poor while widowers become lonely.

Divorced older women and men stand out as particularly disadvantaged in material terms, and they also display the most health-damaging behavior. Because the group of older divorced is likely to grow substantially as new cohorts enter retirement, it seems imperative that the material and social circumstances of this group are assessed continually. In the current elderly population, a mix of causal and selection effects is likely to lie behind the more disadvantaged situation of the divorced. The selection effects are likely to be smaller in later cohorts, where divorce is more common.

What emerges very clearly in Arber's analysis is that gender relations over the life course are transmitted into later life. Women have most often been the upholders of the family's social life and acted as guardians of health-related behavior. Men have provided most of the family's income. These gendered practices are to some extent different in later cohorts, and it will therefore be highly interesting to study the implications for inequalities in later life.

In sum, the contributions to this book illustrate both the variation and the common themes found in different fields within the larger framework of inequality studies. A wide range of inequality outcomes are included, different sets of groups and categories are compared, and explanatory factors are sought at different levels. Nevertheless, a unifying core of assumptions and analytic approaches connects even seemingly remote subject areas.

What lies ahead? It would simply be foolish to try to write an agenda for this overwhelmingly large and unwieldy research field. One key question, however, that unites several of the book's contributions, involves individualization and increased variability versus stability and reproduction. In many respects, it seems the individuals' moorings to families and organizations in the Western world are less stable and strong now than they were some decades ago (Breen 1997). At the same time institutional variability also increases. Contrary to the assumptions of many globalization theories (such as Castells 1996; Martin and Schumann 1997), little or no institutional convergence between the major advanced industrial countries has occurred in the more deregulated world economy since the 1970s (Scharpf and Schmidt 2000; Huber and Stephens 2001; Pierson 2001; Swank 2002). In some respects, it seems that institutional *di*vergence is taking place, for example between continental Europe and the liberal Anglo-Saxon countries. Furthermore, supranational and subnational institutions have added to the already existing national institutional frameworks rather than supplanting them.

It seems to be a highly pertinent question to ask what implications for life chances, life courses, and social mobility such changes could have. Are researchers likely to witness increased individual variation as a result of increased instability and variation at the institutional level? Will families become less important as transmitters of advantage and disadvantage? Will categorical differences in life chances become muted, or will they emerge even stronger, as risk-hedging institutions such as the family and the welfare state become weaker? Analysts of social inequality will have much to do.

References

Blossfeld, Hans-Peter and Rohwer, Götz. 2002. *Techniques of Event History Modeling: New Approaches to Causal Analysis*. Mahwah, N.J.: Lawrence Erlbaum.

Breen, R. 1997. Risk, Recommodification and Stratification. *Sociology* 31:473–489.

Castells, Manuel. 1996. *The Information Age. Vol. 1: The Rise of the Network Society*. Malden, Mass.: Blackwell.

Daly, Mary and Rake, Katherine. 2003. *Gender and the Welfare State: Care, Work and Welfare in Europe and the USA*. Cambridge: Polity.

Erikson, Robert and Jonsson, Jan O. 1996. Explaining Class Inequality in Education: The Swedish Test Case, pp. 1–63 in Erikson, Robert and Jonsson, Jan O. (eds.) *Can Education be Equalized? The Swedish Case in Comparative Perspective*. Boulder, Colo.: Westview.

Goldthorpe, John H. 2000. *On Sociology: Numbers, Narratives, and the Integration of Research and Theory*. Oxford: Oxford University Press.

Granovetter, Mark. 1995. *Getting a Job: A Study of Contacts and Careers*. Chicago: University of Chicago Press.

Hall, Peter A. 1992. The Movement from Keynesianism to Monetarism: Institutional Analysis and British Economic Policy in the 1970s, pp. 90–113 in Steinmo, Sven, Thelen, Kathleen, and Longstreth, Frank (eds.) *Structuring Politics. Historical Institutionalism in Comparative Analyses*. Cambridge: Cambridge University Press.

Hox, J. J. 2002. *Multilevel Analysis: Techniques and Applications*. Mahwah, N.J.: Lawrence Erlbaum.

Huber, Evelyne and Stephens, John D. 2001. *Development and Crisis of the Welfare State: Parties and Policies in Global Markets*. Chicago: University of Chicago Press.

Korpi, Walter and Palme, Joakim. 1998. The Paradox of Redistribution and Strategies of Equality: Welfare State Institutions, Inequality, and Poverty in the Western Countries. *American Sociological Review* 63:661–687.

Levi, Margaret. 1990. A Logic of Institutional Change. Pp. 402–418. In Karen Schweers Cook and Margaret Levi (eds.) *The Limits of Rationality*. Chicago: University of Chicago Press.

Long, J. Scott. 1997. *Regression Models for Categorical and Limited Dependent Variables*. Thousand Oaks, Calif: Sage.

Martin, Hans-Peter and Schumann, Harald. 1997. *The Global Trap: Globalization and the Assault on Prosperity and Democracy*. New York: St. Martin's.

Ni Bhrolcháin, M. 2001. "Divorce Effects" and Causality in the Social Sciences. *European Sociological Review* 17:33–57.

North, Douglass C. 1990. *Institutions, Institutional Change, and Economic Performance*. Cambridge: Cambridge University Press.

Pierson, Paul. 2001. *The New Politics of the Welfare State*. Oxford: Oxford University Press.

Pontusson, J., Rueda, D., and Way, C. R. 2002. Comparative Political Economy of Wage Distribution: The Role of Partisanship and Labour Market Institutions. *British Journal of Political Science* 32:281–308.

Scharpf, Fritz Wilhelm and Schmidt, Vivien Ann. 2000. *Welfare and Work in the Open Economy*. Oxford: Oxford University Press.

Svallfors, Stefan. 2004. *Klassamhällets kollektiva medvetande. Klass och attityder i jämförande perspektiv.* (*The Collective Consciousness of Class Society. Class and Attitudes in Comparative Perspective*). Umeå: Boréa.

Swank, Duane. 2002. *Global Capital, Political Institutions, and Policy Change in Developed Welfare States.* Cambridge: Cambridge University Press.

Tilly, Charles. 1998. *Durable Inequality.* Berkeley, Calif.: University of California Press.

White, Harrison C. 1992. *Identity and Control: A Structural Theory of Social Action.* Princeton, N.J.: Princeton University Press.

CHAPTER TWO

Life Courses and Life Chances in a Comparative Perspective

Karl Ulrich Mayer

If social scientists want to understand how social forces, constraints, and opportunities shape human lives and if they want to go beyond the universal
social conditions of life courses, then three strategies of research can be followed: (1) accounting for within-country differences, (2) tracing historical
changes over time, and (3) comparing patterns of life courses across societies, that is, nation-states.[1] I would like to propose that the latter strategy is
the most suitable one, because it promises to allow unraveling most effectively variations in those generative mechanisms that bring about marked
differences in life course outcomes.

Concentrating on within-country differences will most likely bring to
light conditions that are shared by societies of at least a roughly similar level
of development and that may differ between countries only in their respec-
tive distributions, thus suggesting a focus on compositional effects or what
Arthur Stinchcombe (1987) called "demographic explanations."[2] Concentrating on historical changes over time may not be fruitful if changes over
years or decades are examined as opposed to changes across centuries. And
rarely do researchers have adequate data for the latter comparison, because
societies change very gradually and generally exhibit a high degree of per-
sistence in basic institutions.[3] This should be the case even more when any
changes of conditions within a country concern persons who already have
lived some portion of their lives under the previous conditions.

The very fact that it makes quite a difference into which society one is
born into (or has been adopted into) is hardly disputed. Japanese women
and Russian men differ in their life expectancy by thirty years. And although
social class differentials in mortality are universal, a person can expect to live

17

longer as a lower class Swede than a middle class Brit. Italian men leave their parental home about ten years later than German ones. Japanese and Italian women seem to share the conviction that motherhood should be avoided or delayed rather than rushed into. Retirement can come as early as age 40 for Greek school teachers, or as late as age 59 for German men and 63 for Swedish men. The proportion of young men and women entering the labor market without any vocational training or more than compulsory schooling varied in 1995 between about 10 percent in Germany and about 50 percent in the UK (Solga 2003: 372).

However, what is much less clear, apart from such particular and anecdotal evidence:

1. How do *patterns of life course behaviors and outcomes* vary systematically between societies?
2. How can researchers *attribute observed differences* in such patterns by linking outcomes to varying institutional arrangements, policies, or other conditions?

It is obvious that such a task is quite formidable and would require a satisfactory solution of at least the following problems:

1. Defining a set of properties of life courses such as states, durations, transitions, and risks
2. Demonstrating some degree of internal contingency of these aspects across the lifetime
3. Demonstrating some degree of nonrandomness and systematic covariation, that is, "regimes" between life course aspects in a given society
4. Measuring single aspects or patterns of aspects of the life course in a rigorous and comparable manner
5. Identifying potential explanatory conditions, that is, replacing country names by institutional variables
6. Demonstrating some degree of "coherence" or "regime" between the alleged conditions
7. Showing a sufficient degree of stability of both macro conditions and life course outcomes and their associations
8. Specifying and empirically demonstrating causal linkages between the macro conditions and the observed behaviors and actions with appropriate (micro and process) data

Some assumptions implicit in such an undertaking can quite reasonably be challenged. For instance, it might be doubted whether various life course outcomes for a given individual and across cohorts can be adequately aggregated to make up a meaningful dependent variable or whether they should not be treated as essentially independent from each other. Likewise, analysts might contest the idea that institutional and policy "regimes" are much more than just a *façon de parler* and not rather highly heterogeneous bundles of collective actions and contexts. And, not least, it might be claimed that it is fairly hopeless to expect that social scientists could establish the envisaged macro-micro linkages in a rigorous empirical-dynamic manner rather than— if at all—by mere conceptual and speculative attribution.

Besides the issues about the appropriate levels of aggregation across policies and institutions, across nations, and across life course events and outcomes, there is, in addition, the latent issue of how social scientists should properly understand, conceptualize, and measure the connection between life course structures and processes, life chances, and inequalities.[4]

Why has the interest in cross-national research of life course outcomes increased in recent years? I suggest that this interest has been motivated, among else, by three developments:

1. The major finding of the "Constant Flux" (Erikson and Goldthorpe 1992) of a very similar and fairly robust pattern of social class inheritance has challenged researchers to look at ways of inequality-generating processes and outcomes that in fact might vary more widely between societies than intergenerational class association and for which it therefore might be easier to establish relationships between societal differences and patterns of life chances (Sørensen 1986).

2. Neoliberal calls for enhancing competitiveness and other pressures on labor market regulation, welfare state spending, and programs have raised a renewed interest in how contrasting institutional configurations in different societies would mediate the impact of macroeconomic shocks on inequalities and life chances (Blau and Kahn 2002; DiPrete et al. 2003; Ebbinghaus and Manow 2001a; Hall and Soskice 2001; Scharpf and Schmidt 2000a, 2000b).

3. Demography has assembled a wide array of data on union formation, fertility, and mortality, especially in regard to low fertility and variation in the so-called Second Demographic Transition. At the same time, it has become more clear that the explanations would neither fall out from amassing evermore cross-national aggregate indicators nor from micromodeling individual behavior alone (Esping-Andersen 2002; Hoem 2000; Hoem et al. 2001; Iversen and Rosenbluth 2003; Rosenbluth 2000; Rosenbluth et al. 2002).

Given these interests and the growing availability of both retrospective and prospective longitudinal data, it is hardly surprising that in recent years the body of empirical evidence on cross-national differences in life course outcomes as well as of attempts at explanatory accounts has grown rapidly. My purpose in this chapter is to review the current state of this literature with special attention to claims about explanatory macro conditions. To make this a manageable task, I will rely on empirical evidence from mostly three countries, namely Sweden, (West) Germany, and the United States.

At this point I should make explicit what is meant by "life course outcomes." By the term *life course* sociologists denote the sequence of activities, or states and events, in various life domains spanning from birth to death. The life course is thus seen as the embedding of individual lives into social structures primarily in the form of their partaking in social positions and roles, that is, in regard to their membership in institutional orders. The sociological study of the life course, therefore, aims at mapping, describing, and explaining the synchronic and diachronic distribution of individual persons into social positions across the lifetime. One major aspect of life courses is their internal temporal ordering, that is, the relative duration times in given states as well as the age distributions at various events or transitions. Typically, life course research has covered such domains as educational and training trajectories, family histories, employment trajectories, and occupational careers. Table 2.6 provides an overview of both domains and empirical indicators of life course outcomes.

This chapter is divided into five sections. In the first section I tell a story of how *human development* has evolved from being a field with a highly general and universal bent into something like a *differential life course sociology*. In the second and third sections, I report on initial attempts of mapping first historical and then cross-national variation. In the fourth section, I inspect the institutional configurations and the corresponding life course regimes for Sweden, Germany, and the United States. In the fifth section, I return to the questions raised above, such as whether analysts can expect a macro-sociologically oriented, cross-national life course sociology to persist and flourish as a viable research program.

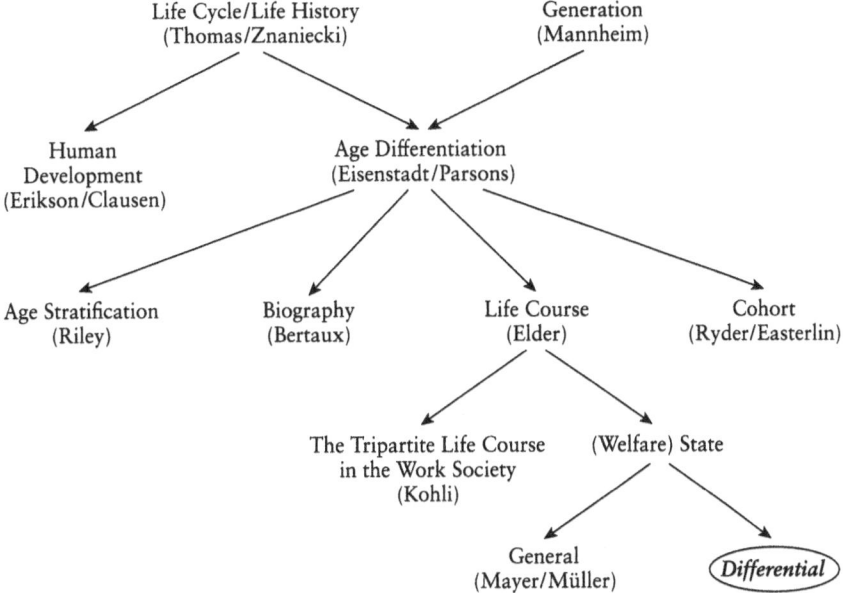

Figure 2.1.   The "Archaeology" of Comparative Life Course Sociology

THE DEVELOPMENT OF LIFE COURSE SOCIOLOGY

Life course sociology emerged and developed over several decades (Figure 2.1). In the years between the two world wars, theoretical notions of development and the life cycle as proposed by psychologists like Charlotte Bühler were not clearly separated from the methodological instrument of life histories (Thomas and Znaniecki 1918) designed to capture personality development, social conditions, and historical context at the same time. In the same period, Karl Mannheim (1928, 1952) proposed another very synthetic concept—the generation—that fused quite general ideas about the social metabolism (that is, social change via the succession of cohorts) with ideas about historical styles and historically specific collective actors.

In the 1940s and 1950s the more psychological traditions of human development (Clausen 1986; Erikson 1980) focusing on internal personal dynamics in mostly group contexts became more clearly distinguished from the sociological concept of age differentiation (Eisenstadt 1964; Parsons 1942) as a structural category. It should be stressed, however, that the close link between psychological, social-psychological, social, and historical perspectives remained a major focus as demonstrated, for instance, in the extensive work of Glen Elder and his associates (1974, 2000).

During the 1960s and 1970s the broader concept of age differentiation was further subdivided by the following concepts:

1. The narrower concept of age stratification (Riley et al. 1994), which stressed not only functional specificity but also inequalities in resource allocation and power
2. Biography as subjective narrative (Bertaux 1981; Kohli 1981)
3. Generation as a cultural construct (Bude 1995)
4. The life course as social structure and institutional patterns (Mayer 1990)
5. The demographic concept of the cohort (Ryder 1965, 1980)

It is worth noting, however, that in almost all of these attempts at concept formation and theory building, the major focus was still on the development of fairly broad universal and general notions. Personal dynamics were now more clearly seen in contrast to diachronic social contexts and historical experiences, and the quest for subjective meaning in life designs and life reviews was pitted against the objectivity of demographic accounts on collective cohorts. Only very slowly, and under the pervasive influence of social historians like Aries (1973), Hareven (1986, 1996), and Modell (Modell et al. 1976; Modell 1991), were variants in the social and cultural organization of life courses postulated and empirically documented.

In the 1980s, researchers made several attempts to pinpoint the specificity of life courses (and biographies) both within and in contrast to past societies. On the one hand, Kohli (1985) and others tried to demonstrate how life courses derive from the prerequisites of (capitalist) economies, where lives and life stages center around work. On the other hand, the uniqueness of modern life courses was derived from the emergence of the welfare state (Mayer and Müller 1986; Mayer and Schoepflin 1989). But even during this stage, very broad categories and dichotomies like "the work society" versus "the welfare state" and "modern" life courses versus "traditional" life courses were the focus of the debate rather than issues related to cross-national and historical variation.

It is, finally, only from the middle half of the 1980s and into the 1990s that something like a "differential" life course sociology developed, that is, descriptions of how patterns of life courses varied between more and more delimited historical periods and between societies. Although rough dichotomies—traditional versus standardized life courses or open versus closed societies—were used at first, gradually more institutional specifics were marshaled. The more detailed the supportive evidence became, the closer social scientists also moved to the question of what accounted for the observed differences. It is my thesis that the development of historical and cross-national comparative life course research opened up the opportunity to come to grips with the mechanisms that might explain how social contexts shape individual life courses.

At this point, it might be useful to be more explicit of what I mean by the term *differential life course*. The term *differential* is used in analogy to the distinction between general and differential psychology, that is, to distinguish between what can be assumed to be universal in human development as an evolutionary product and what differs between individual lives as units of analysis beyond that. This assumption implies a kind of hierarchy where a very basic shared component is universal and evolutionary and, therefore, a mixture of the biological, psychological, and social. On the next level, analysts can imagine a broadly conceptualized historical variability. Then, at each level of historical development researchers can observe differences between countries, although this relationship would only hold if researchers could assume a general path of societal development as postulated in modernization theory. Otherwise historical and societal differences fuse in country-specific path dependencies. Country-specific patterns of life courses (as well as historically specific ones) have to be differentiated according to gender and social class and their interaction. Finally, there will be a residue of inter-individual variation. In this chapter, I assume that the countries are in a fairly similar stage of historical development and concentrate on differences between such societies.[5]

A FIRST STEP: HISTORICAL PHENOMENOLOGY

The initial historical analyses of changes in the social organization of human lives were important in two respects. On the one hand they marshaled evidence and illustration of a wide variety of empirical life course outcomes and their changes over time. For instance, the seminal article by Modell, Furstenberg, and Hershberg (1976) on "Social Change and Transition to Adulthood in Historical Perspective" employed tools of historical demography to map changes in the median ages and age dispersion to argue for the emergence of

TABLE 2.1

Historical Changes in Life Course Regimes

Life Course Regimes	Traditional	Early Industrial	Fordist	Post-Fordist
Unit	Family Farm/Family Firm	Wage Earner	Male Breadwinner, Nuclear Family	Individual
Temporal Organization	Unstable, Unpredictable Discontinuity	Life Cycle of Poverty, Discontinuity	Standardized, Stabilized, Continuity, Progression	Destandardized Discontinuity
Education	Minimal Elementary	Medium Compulsory	Expansion of Secondary, Tertiary Education and Vocational Training	Prolonged, Interrupted, Lifelong Learning
Work	Personal Dependency; Family Division of Labor	Wage Relationship; Firm Paternalism, Unemployment	Full Lifelong Employment; Upward Mobility; Income Progression	Delayed Entry, High Between Firm/Between Occupation Mobility; Flat Income Trajectories, Unemployment
Family	Partial and Delayed Marriage; Instability Due to Death; Property Centered, High Fertility; Early Death	Delayed Universal; Fertility Decline	Early Universal Marriage, Early Childbearing, Medium Fertility	Delayed and Partial Marriage, Pluralized Family Forms, Low Fertility, High Divorce Rate, Sequential Promiscuity
Retirement/ Old Age	With Physical Disability, Old Age Dependency, Early Death	Regulatory or by Disability, Low Pensions	Regulatory: Medium Pensions	Early Retirement; Decreasing Pensions; Increasing Longevity; Increasing Chronic Illness

more distinct life stages and of more regularity and orderliness across time. On the other hand, for the first time they conceived of something like interwoven "life course regimes" where a multitude of events were thought to be the result of a unidirectional logic. This logic was at first derived from the imposition of industrial wage relationships and work discipline (Hareven 1986, 1996) versus the more variable and less predictable patterns of rural lives.

As long as the changes in life course patterns could be thought of as the result of long-term and convergent trends, these fairly vague notions of traditional versus modern and nonstandardized versus standardized life courses did not seem to pose much of a problem and questions of a more precise attribution of the causal mechanisms did not really come to the forefront.

This approach changed only somewhat in the middle of the 1980s, when a number of trends seemed to reverse and a new wave of "destandardization" appeared to increase diversity, delay age at transitions, and increase age dispersion in transitions (Kohli 1987; Held 1986; Buchmann 1989). When it became obvious that simple trend projections and historical dichotomies would hardly be adequate, new tool kits for distinguishing life course regimes were called for. At first this need resulted in developing more fine-graded typologies for different historical periods. Table 2.1 shows a compressed version of one of my own attempts (Mayer 2001) to summarize the literature with a typology for a historical sequence of life course regimes (based among others on Modell et al. [1976], Buchmann [1989], Anderson [1985], Hareven [1986], and Myles [1993]). Life courses here are construed to have developed from a traditional or preindustrial to an early and late industrial type and after that to a postindustrial type, from the Fordist to the post-Fordist life cycle, from the standardized to the destandardized life course.

Under the traditional, preindustrial life course regime, life centered around the family household and its collective survival. Schooling was nonexistent or short (only in winter when children were not needed on the farm), training was part of family socialization in a person's own or other families as servants. Marriage was delayed until either the family farm could be inherited or a farm heiress could be married off or until a sufficient stock of assets could be assembled to establish a household, build a house, or lease land. Life was unpredictable due to the vicissitudes of nature in harvests and the probability of sickness and early death (especially for women in childbirth). Economic dependency and debts were widespread.

The early industrial life course regime is well captured in Rowntree's (1914) image of a life cycle of poverty where industrial workers could only for a short time in their lives rise above poverty when the family was still small and physical working capacity at its peak. Schooling was compulsory but ended at a relatively early age. Dependent work started with ages 12–14 and ended only with physical disability in old age. Marriage was delayed until sufficient resources for establishing a household (furniture, dowry) were accumulated and until employers were prepared to pay a family wage. Unemployment was frequent.

The next stage is postulated to be the industrial, Fordist life course regime. It is characterized by distinct life phases: schooling, training, employment and retirement, stable employment contracts, and long work lives in the same occupation and firm. A living wage for the male breadwinner could allow women to stay at home after marriage. The risks of sickness, unemployment, disability, and old age were covered and softened by an evermore comprehensive system of social insurances. Age at marriage and first birth decreased into the early twenties. Families could accumulate savings to buy their own house or apartment and wages were age-graded. Real incomes and purchasing power increased for a good part of the working life and then stabilized until retirement when pensions and low rents or mortgage payments ensured a standard of living comparable to the one of the active years. Relative affluence allowed children to receive more education and training than the parental generation, and parents could afford to support their children in buying their own homes. The life course matched the logic of the division of labor within the nuclear family and of the family welfare as a joint utility function of the family members. Social identities were well defined and stable. The middle class expanded and workers were integrated into society socially, economically, and politically.

The standardized linear and homogeneous life course that emerged in post-World War II society is generally attributed to the coming together of two forces: Fordist industrial mass production in which a moderate wage, relatively secure working class became established as the "universal" class, and the welfare state's guarantee of income across the entire life cycle of the family. The standardization of the life course meant in a sense that workers' life chances became "middle class."

The postindustrial, post-Fordist life course regime in contrast can be characterized by increasing destandardization across the lifetime and increasing differentiation and heterogeneity across the population. Education has expanded in level and duration, and vocational and professional training as well as further training have proliferated. A number of life transitions have been delayed, prolonged, and increased in age variance, and the extent of universality and of orderly sequences has decreased. Entry into employment has become more precarious. First work contracts are often temporary. Employment interruptions due to unemployment, resumed education or training, or other times out of the labor force have increased. The rate of job shifts increase, and occupations are increasingly not held lifelong. Careers become highly contingent on the economic fates of the employing firms; therefore, heterogeneity across working lives increases. Downward career mobility increases relative to upward career opportunities. Working lives shorten due to later entry and frequent forced early retirement. The experience of unemployment becomes widespread, but concentrates on women, foreign workers, young people, and older workers. Age at marriage has increased. Nonmarital unions exploded and became a normal phase before marriage. Parenthood is delayed and for a significant number of couples never comes about. Divorce increases as well as the number of children growing up in a single-parent household or without a father present in the household. Women overtake men in their share of general education and greatly increase their occupational qualifications. Women want to work lifelong, and they have to work to augment the family budget or support themselves as single mothers. The standard of living in old age is threatened by reduced pension entitlements. The relation between the home and the workplace is changing rapidly. Women are out of the house most of the day.

Although such a historical phenomenology of life course changes may be more or less plausible, it remains unclear what actually are the precise mechanisms and institutional underpinnings that would generate the distinct life course outcomes. A reading of the literature produces a list like the following one:

1. The traditional life course regime was regulated by the demographics of high mortality and high fertility, by prerequisites and vicissitudes of a rural economy without the benefits of the agrochemical fertilization of soil and scientific animal husbandry.

2. The early industrial life course regime was subjected to an untamed capitalist economy with a weak labor movement and—due to the first demographic transition—a high supply of labor.

3. The late industrial life course regime was made possible by effective co-ordination between capital and labor, mass production and mass consumption, macroeconomic policy intervention stabilizing economic cycles, full employment, rising real wages and standards of living, and, finally, welfare state expansion.

4. For the postindustrial life course regime (or rather life course disorder), a manifold of major causal conditions have been identified: educational expansion and its unintended effects, women's movement, value changes, individualization and self-direction, weakness of trade unions, deindustrialization, the labor market crises with spiraling structural unemployment, globalization of economic markets, and the demographic crunch produced by the low levels of fertility and a prolonged life span.

Mayer and Hillmert (2003) in a recent paper have juxtaposed a stylized history of institutional discontinuity and life course changes for Germany for the period from 1960 to 2000 with empirical observations on life course patterns of cohorts born between 1950 and 1971. Table 2.2 shows a selection of indicators. The median age at leaving home shows a remarkable similarity across time for both men and women from the 1970s to the 1990s. The median age at marriage exhibits the well-known massive rise by about five years up to the 1990s, when it stabilized. Age at first job increased in a trend-like fashion by about three years for both women and men. Job durations and occupational stability, which should have been most affected by the "postindustrial crisis," appear to be fluctuating. What analysts can observe then with such data on transitions to adulthood, employment trajectories, and family behavior appears to be a mixture of robust trends and non-trend-like cohort variation, but scarcely any indication of the dramatic consequences of a "regime change," such as the breakdown of the Rhenish model postulated in the political economy literature.

These historical typologies are not only at best partially empirically cor-roborated but also suffer from the same weakness as the parallel and related tradition of intercohort comparisons (Modell et al. 1976; Mayer 1994, 1995; Mayer and Huinink 1993). "Cohorts" or "historical periods" mark differences, but the assumptions as to what causes such differences remain foggy. The holistic assumption of overall regulation regimes resulting in specific patterns of life course outcomes like "the golden age, "Fordism," and "post-Fordism" is more postulated than proven (Boyer and Durand 1997; Myles 1993). Moreover, it is apparent that the assumed trends or period differences can claim little general validity as to specific timing, turning points,

TABLE 2.2
Selected Life Course Indicators (in Years) for
West Germans Born 1950–1971

Birth Cohort	1950	1955	1960	1964	1971
Median Age at Leaving Home: Men	25	24	23	23	24
Median Age at Leaving Home: Women	22	21	21	21	22
Median Age at First Marriage: Men	25	27	30	29	—[a]
Median Age at First Marriage: Women	21	23	26	26	—[b]
Median Age (First Job): Men	18.8	19.5	19.9	20.3	21.1
Median Age (First Job): Women	18.1	18.9	19.7	20.3	20.9
Median Age (First Stable Job): Men	20.2	21.3	21.7	21.8	23.9
Median Age (First Stable Job): Women	19.0	20.0	21.0	21.7	22.3
Median Job Duration (First Stable Job): Men	4.3	5.3	5.3	6.6	5.5
Median Job Duration (First Stable Job): Women	4.6	4.8	5.2	5.3	5.3
Median Occupational Duration (First Stable Job): Men	>9	>11	>9	13.1	>8
Median Occupational Duration (First Stable Job): Women	6.2	7.7	7.6	7.4	6.4

First stable job: minimum duration of two years

[a] At the time of interviewing at the age of 27, less than 25 percent have married

[b] 25 percent have married up to age 24, but less than 50 percent up to age 27

Data: German Life History Study; West Germany and German citizens only; 1950 = 1949–51; 1955 = 1954–56; 1960 = 1959–61

and direction. Not least, all cross-referencing of "periods" and "life course regimes" are faced with the difficulty that the lifetimes of individuals are likely to extend beyond postulated period boundaries. Women and men may have experienced their childhood in one period, their formative years in another, and their retirement in a third. Attributing the whole or even larger parts of lives to any single period and their concomitant institutional impacts must therefore run into insurmountable obstacles.

Cross-national comparisons (and intra-country developments) promise (partial) remedies in both respects and may allow for a better understanding of the mechanisms bringing about varying patterns of life course outcomes.

WELFARE REGIMES, VARIETIES OF CAPITALISM, AND LIFE COURSE OUTCOMES

The first take on overall cross-national life course regimes was based on dichotomies. However, these dualistic cross-national typologies were connected with more explicit arguments of how institutional arrangements and life course outcomes might be causally linked. One example (Mayer 1997) took its clues from David Soskice's (1991) microeconomic analyses of cross-national differences in training systems and industrial financing as well as from Aage Sørensen's distinction between open and closed position systems (1990) (Figure 2.2).

Life courses in *liberal market* (deregulated, open) societies are postulated to be based on social relationships that are invested with comparatively little advance of trust. As a consequence, they are based on a low degree of mutual obligation and tend to be temporary. The state stays to a large extent outside the contractual relations between employers and workers. It does not assume much responsibility on the areas of vocational training. Individual and firm investments in training are therefore small. There is no quality standardization and no formal degrees and certificates accepted across firms. The transition between school and gainful employment leads to a series of partly marginal employment interrupted by phases of unemployment or being out of the labor force. Jobs are not so clearly defined, and shifts between jobs are common. Loyalty to one specific firm is low. There are fewer career positions within companies, and career ladders are shorter, which in the aggregate should result in rather flat income trajectories. In the absence of seniority schemas and efficiency wages, incomes should be relatively closely tied to perceived productivity.

In such a context, actors have to be keen to maximize their short-term returns. Workers maximize their wages at the expense of job security and the quality of working conditions, while employers maximize profits and minimize investment in human capital. Similar short-term orientations pervade family life. The position in the labor market is consequential for family commitments and stability. Because affluence is preferred to security, decisions regarding marriage and divorce are more closely tied to income expec-

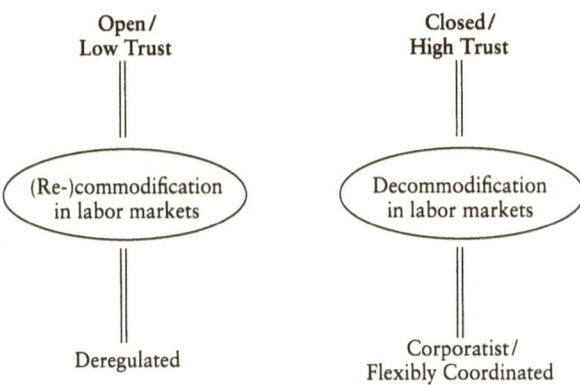

Figure 2.2. Dualistic Life Course Regimes

tations. Because families are less of a joint project, marriages are easier to enter and easier to dissolve. Because there are few safeguards against income loss in cases of divorce or for children born out of wedlock, divorced women and single mothers more often have to choose to marry or remarry to avoid poverty. Such contexts are highly predictive even for seemingly unrelated areas of behavior: youth is not well integrated into society, onset of sexual intercourse is low, and juvenile delinquency is high (Breen and Buchmann 2002) (see Table 2.3).

In contrast, life courses in *flexibly coordinated* (closed, corporatist) societies are characterized by higher levels of mutual trust and therefore lead to more long-term commitments. Strong trade unions and employers' associations as well as closer community ties and a more active role of the state are at the basis of these high trust relationships. Investments in vocational training by young workers are facilitated, because the return of employment and higher incomes is highly likely. Conversely, companies are prepared to invest in training because they can expect that workers remain in the firm for a sufficient length of time. The formal rights of unions and work councils make layoffs costly. Between-firm shifts are predominantly voluntary. Technological and organizational restructuring are managed not via layoffs, but rather through the natural turnover of workers. Even in the case of manufacturing downsizing, the state tends to take over some responsibility to ease manpower shrinkage. Moderate or even minimal wage increases are acceptable, because a lot of life risks are covered by welfare provisions and no

TABLE 2.3

Political Economies: Deregulated and Coordinated

	Deregulated Market Economies	Coordinated Market Economies
Prime Examples	USA, UK	Germany, Austria, Netherlands
Financial/Economic Governance	Short-Term Financial Markets; Equity Financing; Limited Business Coordination; Antitrust Laws	Long-Term Financial Capital; Debt Financing; Strong Business Associations; Intercompany Networks
Production System	Low-Skill Production; Mass Products; Numeric Flexibilization	High-Skill Production; High-Quality Products; Flexible Specialization
Labor Relations	Decentralized Bargaining; Contentious Workplace Relations; Low Trust/Coordination	Coordinated Bargaining; Statutory Worker Representation; High Trust/Coordination
Schooling and Training	General Education; On-the-Job Training; Low Coordination Between Schools and Employers/Unions	Vocational Training; Strong Coordination Between Schools and Employers/Unions
Labor Market Regulation	Minimalist State; Weak Employment Protection; Low/Short-Term Unemployment Benefits; Low (flat) Pensions	Interventionist State; Strong Employment Protection; High/Long-Term Unemployment Benefits; High (Earnings-Related) Pensions
Job/Mobility Structure	"Individualist Mobility Regime" Short Tenure; High Turnover; Rewards Structure Tied to Individual Skills/Productivity	"Collectivist Mobility Regime" Long Tenure; Low Turnover; Reward Structure Tied to Characteristics of Job Positions
Occupational Careers	Stop-Gap Labor Market Entry; Short Tenure; High Turnover; Unstable, High Interfirm Job Shifts; Upward/Downward Mobility	Smooth Labor Market Entry; Long Tenure; Low Turnover; Stable, Low Interfirm Job Shifts; Mostly Upward Mobility
Income Mobility	Flat; High Variance; High Poverty	Progressive; Low Variance; Low/Moderate Poverty
Retirement	Late Retirement; Low Replacement; High Inequality in Old Age	Early Retirement; High Replacement; Medium Inequality in Old Age
Family Structure	Unstable; High Divorce; Gender Equality	Stable; Low Divorce; Male Dominated

SOURCES: Allmendinger and Hinz 1998; Ebbinghaus 2002; Mayer 1997, 2001; Soskice 1991.

reserves have to be built up for training and education of children, for illness, unemployment, and old age.

A higher degree of trust also regulates the family sphere. Although relationships between partners are increasingly entered on the basis of equality, families are still joint projects and not the mere agglomerates of individual life designs. Such life courses are embedded in regional and local milieus and relatively integrated family networks. Youth tend to be well integrated into society and transition into employment is mostly well structured, sexual maturity is delayed, and juvenile delinquency is relatively lower.

In these two ideal types of life courses, in *deregulated* and *flexibly coordinated societies*, the linkages between the macro-institutional structures and individual life courses are primarily construed as mutually influencing incentive systems. Historically, given institutional differences shape the detailed regulations, reciprocal relationships, and policies across various life domains and life phases, and influence motives and orientations of individual actors. Across the life course, early influences shape and direct later trajectories in a cumulative manner. On such a basis, social scientists can expect stabilizing and homogenizing tendencies across the life course and across population groups in flexibly coordinated societies whereas in liberal market societies diverging fortunes would result in greater overall lifetime inequalities.

However, any such attempt to collapse both institutional configurations and life course regimes into a neat comprehensive dichotomy must encounter fatal problems. The crucial institutional building blocks of educational systems, education-labor market linkages, labor market regulations, social insurance provisions, and family policies defy such easy reductionism in regard to macro contexts. It was, therefore, tempting to look for more differentiated typologies that still retained the assumption of institutional "ensembles," "configurations," or "regimes" (Figure 2.3).

Three such proposals played an important role:

1. Esping-Andersen's first three and then four "worlds of welfare capitalism" (1990, 1999);
2. The "varieties of capitalism" literature based on the convergence of modes of macroeconomic coordination, production systems, and employment relations (Crouch 2001; Crouch and Streeck 1997; Hall and Soskice 2001; Ebbinghaus and Manow 2001b);
3. Typologies of welfare state policies (Leisering and Leibfried 1999; Leisering 2003).

TABLE 2.4

Welfare State Regimes and Institutional Configurations/Life Courses

	Liberal Market State	Continental Conservative Welfare State	Scandinavian Social Democratic Welfare State	Southern European Welfare State
Unit	Individual	Family	Individual	Family
Temporal Organization	Discontinuity, Destandardized	Continuity, Standardized	Continuity, Standardized	Continuity, Destandardized
Inequalities: Heterogeneity	High, Dualism: Private Protection/Excluded, Gender Equality	Medium, Male Dominance	Low, Homogeneity, Gender Equality	High, Male Dominance
Intra Cohort/Time Inequalities	Unstable, Cumulative, and High Inequality	Stable, Medium Inequalities Insiders/Dependents/Outsiders	Stable, Equality	Unstable, Cumulative, and High Inequality

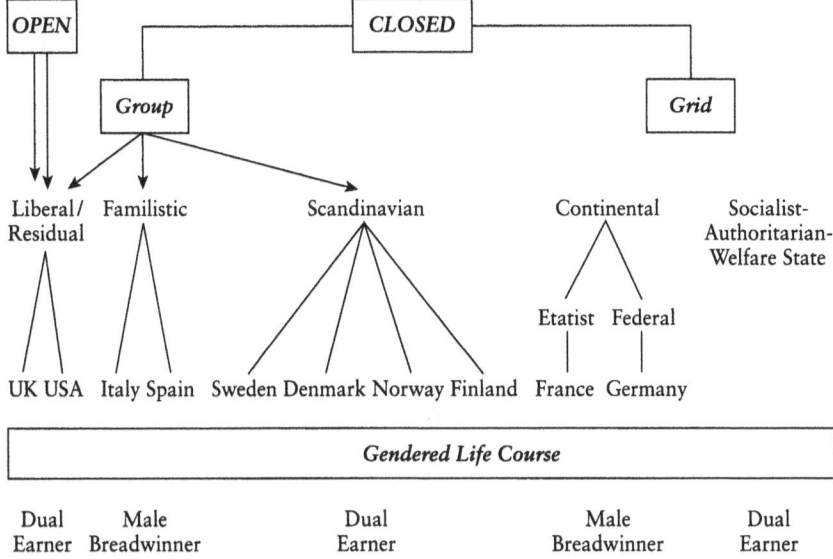

Figure 2.3.   Life Course Regimes: Cross-National Typologies

Several cross-national comparisons of specific life course outcomes have summarized their findings by the help of one of these schemata, but primarily that of welfare state regimes (e.g., Blossfeld and Hakim 1997; Blossfeld and Drobnic 2001; Leisering and Leibfried 1999; Mayer 2001; Mills and Blossfeld 2003). And a plausible argument can be made that major institutions[6] and a series of life course outcomes do in fact cluster to a considerable extent (Mayer 2001) (see Table 2.4).

FROM COUNTRY "REGIMES" TO NATIONS AND POLICIES

However useful such overviews might be as interpretative summaries, life course outcomes are not conditioned on welfare "regimes" or varieties of political economies, but rather on the concrete specifics of particular institutional rules and incentive systems (Blossfeld 2003). Therefore, aggregating countries must introduce ambiguities that undermine the uses of such schemata in developing causal hypotheses about life course outcomes. This premise becomes even more apparent in a time when countries selectively change their social policies and labor market regulations. To give just a few examples, France and Germany differ markedly in their provisions for childcare. The United States and the UK are worlds apart in their levels of health insurance coverage. They also differ in the way they channel youth into the labor market. The United States has a higher proportion of school dropouts than the UK, and the UK has gradually developed an increasing variance in general schooling levels attained (Hillmert 2001). Not least, the United States is unique in incarcerating a fifth of its male black population for a considerable time of their young adult years (Pettit and Western 2004). Austria and Germany differ in the extent of non–firm-based vocational training.

If cross-national life course research wants to succeed in establishing credible links between institutional antecedents, the timing of life course transitions, and the distribution of life chances, then there is no alternative than to resort to the level of particular countries and particular institutions.

In Table 2.5 I have listed the institutional configurations for the United States, Germany, and Sweden and I have made an attempt to summarize in Table 2.6 the research literature on what researchers currently know about life course outcomes. Below I cut across the order of sequence in the tables and selectively connect given institutions and life course behavior and thereby suggest specific causal linkages.[7]

In the United States, universal and comprehensive schooling without institutionalized apprenticeships make for a fairly standardized age at leaving secondary school around 17 (with a non-negligible rate of high school dropouts). Labor market entry comes early even for college graduates, but the transition between education and full labor market integration is often marked by a sequence of stop-gap jobs (Allmendinger 1989a, 1989b; Oppenheimer and Kalmijn 1995). Low-paid and marginal employment as well as unemployment is widespread among young workers. Moreover, even starting in high school and continuing through college, full-time education and work are frequently combined. Educational certificates are of minor importance, occupational identities are weak, and therefore work lives are primarily structured by individual attempts to make good earnings. Commitment to given firms is low, and job shifts between firms are frequent. Deregulated labor markets foster employment, but depress and polarize wages. Mean income trajectories are fairly flat across working lives because efficiency wages and seniority premiums are weak, and effects of the business cycle are stronger than age effects. Labor income inequality is high, and the stability of relative income positions across the working life is low. Employment opportunities for women are relatively better and employment trajectories are more continuous, but women's work is hardly optional, because their share in the family budget is badly needed. Therefore, women's full-time rather than part-time work is the standard (Blossfeld and Hakim 1997). Probably because of the relative economic independence of women, divorce rates are high, but so are remarriage rates of women with children, who could hardly cope otherwise. Nonetheless and despite bad family allowances and services, fertility among these countries is not at the lowest. At retirement, the replacement rate of pension income compared to the final wages is relatively low. There is a high variance of the median age at retirement, because on the one hand, older workers can be fired easily, and on the other hand, older workers continue to work even at lower wages because of the low level of expected pension income. What are the major risks in this life course regime: low skills, low wages, and being working poor—below or close to the poverty level. For a considerable proportion of people, the threat of a cumulative cycle of disadvantage is very real.

(West) Germany stratifies school and training tracks and thus induces a higher variance at the ages at which young adults leave the formative period. A prolonged educational period also pushes the age of entry into the labor market upward. Because training is dominantly organized in the dual system, transitions to employment are smoother and integrated along the lines of occupational tracks. Training investments by both firms and young people are high, and therefore the attainment and the later use of certified skills play a large role in young people's lives. About 40 percent add an additional training period after the first concluded training, but most of that is an orderly progression in the same occupational domain (Jacob 2003). Job shifts between firms are rare (but increasing for men), and changes between fields of occupational activities are even rarer (Mayer and Hillmert 2003). For those who successfully manage their labor market entry, mean income trajectories are progressive up to the early forties and then flatten out. Efficiency wages and seniority schemes are widespread even in the private sector. The industry-wide binding character of collective agreements and informal wage coordination between industry unions ensures relatively low degrees of wage inequality. Labor market rigidities go hand in hand with high rates of unemployment, especially for younger workers of foreign descent and women. But primarily older workers become laid off and can transit from unemployment to early retirement at age 60. Although the labor force participation of women has been increasing rapidly, the career opportunities and

TABLE 2.5

National Institutional Configurations

Life Course Institutions	United States	Germany	Sweden
Schooling	Low Stratification, Low Standardization, General Education	Highly Stratified, High Standardization	Low Stratification, High Standardization
Vocational Training	Marginalized Vocational School, On-the-Job Training	Apprentice/Vocational School, Dual System, Highly Standardized, Employer/Union Coordinated	Vocational School (Upper Secondary), Unstandardized, Uncoordinated
School-to-Work Linkages	Loose Linkages, Personal Networks	Tight Linkages, Apprenticeships, Employment Offices	Loose Linkages, Labor Exchange
Production Systems	Low Skill, Mass Products, High External Flexibility, Service-Based Economy	High Skill, Export-Oriented, High-Quality Niche, High Internal Flexibility	High Skill, Export-Oriented
Labor Relations Systems	Decentralized Bargaining, Low Union Density, Contentious Relations	Coordinated (sectoral) Bargaining Encompassing Employer Association, Medium Union Density, Cooperative Relations	Coordinated (sectoral) Bargaining Encompassing Employer Association, High Union Density
Firm-Based Institutions	Weak Internal Labor Markets, High Occupational Welfare	Strong Internal Labor Markets, Medium Occupational Welfare	Weak Internal Labor Markets, Low Occupational Welfare
Welfare State (General)	Low Decommodification; Means-Tested Benefits; Mixed Services; Flat Benefits	Medium Decommodification; Employment-Related Benefits; Transfer Payments; Contribution Related	High Decommodification; Universal Benefits; Public Services; Redistributional

	Low	Medium	High
Public Sector	Low	Medium	High
Active Labor Market Policy	Low	(Medium) Training/Employment Subsidies	High Vocational (Re)Training; Low Skill Public Employment
Labor Market Regulation	Deregulated, Weak Job Protection	Highly Regulated, Work Conditions and Benefits, Strong Job Protection	Medium Regulation, Work Conditions and Benefits, Weak Job Protection
Retirement/Pensions	Flat Social Security; Partial Firm Pensions; Pre-Tax Pensions Savings	Dual System: Earnings Related Pensions; High Level Company-Based Supplement	Two-Tiered: Flat Universal and Supplemental Earnings Related; Early Exit Schemes; Long-Term Unemployment/Disability
System of Taxation	Low Level of Taxation, Unit = Individual (Dual Earner Model)	Moderate Level of Taxation, Unit = Household (Male-Breadwinner Model)	High Levels of Taxation, Unit = Individual (Dual Earner Model)
Family Policies: Family Allowance, Childcare, Parental Leave	No Family Allowance; Privatized Child Care; Short, Job Protection; Zero Income Replacement	Direct Cash Transfer – Entitled to Household Head; Low Public Childcare, Half-day Schooling; Short Income Replacement; Long Job Protection	Direct Cash Transfer to Child; Strong Public Provision of Childcare; Long/Generous Income Replacement and Job Protection

TABLE 2.6
National Life Course Outcomes

	United States	Germany	Sweden
Leaving Home	Early, High Variance	Medium, High Variance	Early, Low Variance
Age Leaving School/ Training	Early, Unstratified	Late, Highly Stratified	Medium, Unstratified
Labor Market Entry	Early, Loosely Coordinated Stop-Gap, General Skills	Late, Highly Coordinated, Industry-Specific Skills	Medium, Moderately Coordinated, General Skills
Economic Self-Sufficiency	Early, Earnings	Late	Early, Earnings + Study Grants/Welfare Transfers
Family Formation	Early Entry into Marriage/Parenthood	Cohabitation Before Marriage, Delayed Entry into Marriage/ Partial Parenthood	High Permanent Cohabitation, Delayed Entry into Marriage/Parenthood
Job Shifts	High Intrafirm Mobility, High Interfirm Mobility	Moderate Intrafirm Mobility, Low Interfirm Mobility	High Intrafirm Mobility, High Interfirm Mobility
Worklife Class Mobility	High, Upward and Downward	Low, Upward	Intermediate, Upward

Employment / Unemployment	High Employment, Continuous/Frictional Unemployment, Early Entry/Late Exit	Low Employment, Low Youth Unemployment, Prolonged Unemployment, Late Entry/Early Exit	High Employment, Continuous/Frictional Unemployment, High Youth Unemployment, Late Entry/Late Exit
Careers of Women	High Participation, High Qualifications Variance, Mostly Full Time, Continuous	Medium Participation, Medium Homogeneous Qualifications, Mostly Part Time, Interrupted	High Participation, Low + High Qualifications, Full Time/Part Time, Continuous
Family Life Course	Unstable, High Single Mothers, Medium Fertility	Stable, Low Single/ Nonmarital Parenthood, Low Fertility	Moderately Stable, High (Single)/Nonmarital Parenthood, Medium/ Declining Fertility
Income Trajectories	Flat, High Variance, High Poverty	Progressive, Low Variance, (Low) Poverty	Flat, Low Variance, Low Poverty
Retirement	Late Exit, High Variance, Low Replacement, High Inequality in Old Age	Early Exit, Low Variance, High Replacement, Medium Income Inequality	Gradual Late Exit, Medium Variance, High Replacement, Low Income Inequality

commitments for married women with younger children are greatly limited. Career interruptions in the early years after childbirth and later part-time work are normatively expected and institutionally supported by restricted childcare and child leave options (Mayer 2003). Marriages are comparatively stable, but fertility is low. Especially for women with higher education, a dualistic behavior pattern is observable: both high career commitment with no children or career withdrawal and two children (Huinink 1995). Retirement comes early because firms try to get rid of older workers with higher wages, but this practice is increasingly limited by tighter disability and old age pension rules. The major life course risks in (West) Germany are long-term unemployment and being pushed into the group of labor market outsiders.

Life courses in Sweden are distinct, especially in the following regard: the full-time, full working life integration of women into the labor force, a somewhat higher level of fertility until the early 1990s, the permanency of nonmarital unions, effective policies of labor market integration especially for younger workers (with the result of early leaving of the parental home), and, finally, late legal and relatively later actual ages at retirement. The major life course risks are the transitions from comprehensive school to employment with now high levels of youth unemployment or enrollment in employment policy measures, and the entrapment into low wage, low skill employment in the public sector for women. (Note, however, that Korpi and Mertens [2003] have challenged the traditional wisdom about the higher labor market integration capacity of the German system of dual training in comparison with Sweden.) There is then the risk of "welfare careers" both inside and outside the employment system.

These life course regimes can be summarized along four dimensions:

1. Which is the action unit around which life courses are primarily organized?
2. What is the predominant temporal organization of states and events across the lifetime?
3. How heterogeneous and unequal are life courses between social classes and between men and women?
4. How do inequalities within birth cohorts develop across their collective lifetime?

In the United States, the basic unit and actor in life courses is the individual. The organization of lifetime is not well standardized, and it exhibits a fair degree of discontinuity. Income inequalities both in a cross-sectional and lifetime perspective are high and unstable. Income inequalities are accentuated by highly unequal and dualistic access to health and incomes after retirement. Those who can afford private insurance are well covered, and those who cannot afford private insurance are at risk of falling into poverty. The high labor market integration of women in contrast tends to favor equality between men and women. The relative income position across the life course is quite unstable, but still tends to result in cumulative cycles of privilege and disadvantage and thus increasing inequality across the life course.

Germany still organizes life courses around the nuclear family, although with increasing shares of lifetime spent outside conventional families. In comparison, life courses are still highly continuous and standardized. Cross-sectional inequalities are in the medium range and fairly stable across work life and retirement. Inequalities, however, increase between those integrated into the highly protected labor market and those who either have a hard time entering or are being phased into early retirement via temporary unemployment or are being kept out (at least partially in lifetime and in working hours) as in the case of women. Some of these outsiders are cushioned by social wages and others by their families. Gender inequalities decrease somewhat—most in general education, occupational training, and tertiary education, less in employment, and much less in occupational careers. These gains are threatened, though, when external economic pressures increase, and risks are disproportionately shared by women and foreigners.

Sweden favors the individual woman and man as the unit and agent of the life course—not least through its tax system and by shifting some of the burdens of women's caring work to public social services. Its still very high degree of social protection supports the continuity across life, and this tends to standardize life courses. The income distribution is still quite equitable and transfer incomes stabilize and equalize income trajectories.

One conclusion from this discussion seems inescapable: Aggregating on the side of countries as independent variables in explaining and understanding life course outcomes is not a good strategy. Although summary interpretative contrasts between, say, liberal countries like the United States or the UK, and conservative-corporatist countries like Germany and the Netherlands may be useful, the aggregation into families of countries, in general, does not facilitate the identification of the underlying mechanisms. Also, for given countries only disaggregating between fairly specific institutional rules and incentives make it possible to formulate adequate causal hypotheses about nationally variable life course behavior. In other words, the analytical and empirical work has to be accomplished on the subnational level, while more lofty interpretative generalizations might—with increasing risks of oversimplification—venture beyond that.

CAN THE ASSUMPTION OF NATIONAL "LIFE COURSE REGIMES" BE MAINTAINED?

The necessary next step is to go beyond establishing the covariation between the array of institutions and policies, on the one hand, and the corresponding behavioral distributions, on the other hand. What social scientists are looking for are the mechanisms that channel individual actors in specific directions, expose them to variable risks and opportunities, and let them respond to given incentive systems. However, analysts must then confront the question of whether, after the deconstruction of ensembles of countries, the assumption of "life course regimes" as a meaningful comprehensive response to nationally specific institutions and policies has to be given up. I will use three examples to illustrate some of the issues involved: exit to retirement, the interaction of different outcomes across the life course, and the relationship between life course risks and risk compensation.

Ebbinghaus (2002: passim and 175 and 176) in his recent comparative study on "Exits to Retirement" has documented the political struggles and policy changes that have effectively impacted median ages of retirement and participation in early retirement schemes. In Germany, the trade unions and the employers associations collude to externalize the costs of economic restructuring by strongly supporting legal schemes allowing early retirement with low penalties in pension levels. The government opened the possibility for older unemployed workers to receive an old age pension after age 59 in order to reduce the unemployment figures.[8] These policies are attractive for older voters, but increased the financial burden of old age social security already stretched by reduced contributions (due to unemployment) and population aging. Despite upward changes in the legal ages of retirement, this policy resulted in a median age of retirement of 59 for men and 60 for women. The probabilities of exiting from work, however, still peak at legal ages, that is, 63 and 65 for men and 60 and 63 for women. In Sweden, full employment policies are intended to keep older workers in their jobs as long as possible. As a result, median ages of retirement are highest and the age variance is highly compressed in Sweden in comparison to other European countries. Both men and women have the highest probability of exiting from work at age 65. In Sweden part-time, partial retirement was popular and reached up to a quarter of all eligible workers, although it is gradually being phased out. In the United States, social security as a base pension is low and only available after age 65. Therefore, actual ages at retirement vary greatly with access to employer-controlled private pension plans and the ability of workers to benefit from tax-deductible pension savings. Although employment levels of the 60–64-year-olds are as high or even higher than in Sweden and much higher (in comparison) for those above age 65, the United States is the only country where legal changes in age rules of access to social security (and most recently probably also the dramatic loss of pensions entitlements on the stock market) have reversed the trend to earlier retirement. Thus, in the example of retirement, researchers can very convincingly document that, although the motives of employers to shed their older workforce and the motives of workers and employees to retire early (if the replacement rate of the pension is acceptable) are quite similar across societies, these dispositions are transformed into variable outcomes by nationally varying pension policies, electoral strategies, employment policies, and the strength of trade unions.

If a good case (in good case studies) can be made as to how specific institutional macro configurations translate into specific life course outcomes, this still leaves open the question of how different aspects of the life course interconnect and whether such interactions vary between nations. Jonsson and Mills (2001: xii–xxiv) in the first comprehensive life course study in Sweden report three such interactions where Sweden clearly breaks away from expected patterns. In the first instance, it is observed that Swedish women, in contrast to most other countries, do not suffer career setbacks even after relatively extended periods of maternity leave. Furthermore, union dissolution does not seem to impact negatively on women's career development—but, in fact, it has the opposite effect of triggering career advancement. And, finally, again—in stark contrast to other countries—single mothers in Sweden do enjoy just as many educational opportunities as other women and do not experience higher rates of poverty. These three examples show how the workings of the Swedish welfare state do not just effect separate outcomes, but also the interaction of various life course outcomes.

TABLE 2.7
Life Course Risks and Mobility Regimes

	United States	Germany	Sweden
Occupational Mobility (Males)	Unstable; High Mobility; Upward and Downward	Stable; Low Mobility	Intermediate; High Mobility; Upward Mobility
Household Level Income Mobility	Moderate Relative Mobility/ High Absolute Mobility	High Relative Mobility/ Moderate Absolute Mobility	High Relative Mobility/ Moderate Absolute Mobility
Union Dissolution	High Rate; Intermediate Risk of Poverty	Low Rate; High Risk of Poverty	Moderate Rate; Low Risk of Poverty
	Weak Welfare Protection; High Female Labor Force Participation Rate; Moderate Repartnering Rates	Moderate Welfare Protection; Low Female Labor Force Participation Rate; Moderate Repartnering Rates	Strong Welfare Protection; High Female Labor Force Participation Rate; Rapid Repartnering Rates
Job Displacement	Moderate Rate of Job Loss; Low Risk Long-Term Unemployment; Moderate Risk of Wage Loss; Moderate Risk of Poverty	Moderate Rate of Job Loss; High Risk Long-Term Unemployment; Low Risk of Wage Loss; Low/Moderate Risk of Poverty	Moderate Rate of Job Loss; Low Risk Long-Term Unemployment; Low Risk of Wage Loss; Low Risk of Poverty
	Low Replacement/ Short-Term Unemployment Benefits; Secondary Earner	Generous/Long-Term Un-employment Benefits; Insider-Outsider Labor Market; No Secondary Earner	Generous/Medium-Term Unemployment Benefits; Secondary Earner
Poverty Dynamics	High Rate of Entry; Low Rate of Exit	Moderate Rate of Entry; Moderate Rate of Exit	Low Rate of Entry; High Rate of Exit
Mobility Regime	Weak (dis)Incentives; Weak Insurance	Incentive-Based System	Insurance-Based System

SOURCE: DiPrete (2002)

In a recent paper on "Life Course Risks, Mobility Regimes, and Mobility Consequences," DiPrete (2002) examines the risks given societies typically allow their members to be exposed to, on the one hand, and the assistance and compensation societies provide once their members experience adverse events, on the other hand (Table 2.7). Looking at unemployment, the effect of union dissolution on poverty and occupational mobility, DiPrete shows that Germany has well-functioning institutional provisions to protect from income or status losses, but, if they occur nonetheless, the provisions only partially compensate for such losses by social security measures. Its occupationally segregated labor markets enhance employment stability but restrict access to jobs, and thus lead to high and relatively long-term unemployment. The rate of union dissolution is lower than in either the United States or Sweden, but—surprisingly—welfare losses are relatively higher after divorce. Although court settlements are relatively generous, they cannot offset (or might even counteract) the advantages of high employment participation. Sweden, in contrast, allows negative events to occur at relatively higher rates (more in the family sphere, less in the labor market), but very effectively compensates for income losses by supporting labor market integration. As a result, income and class position are relatively stable across the life course. The United States neither protects well from adverse life events (high divorce rates, high downward mobility, high layoffs, high poverty rate) or from low paying jobs, nor does it offer much assistance in such cases of need. Thus, the distinctive profiles of life course outcomes can be directly traced to the institutional settings in the three countries. Across various life course outcomes, institutions differentially define rules and act as incentive or disincentive systems, impact on the incidence of risks, and administer selective compensation in case of negative life events.

DiPrete's analysis, then, is an encouraging demonstration that by focusing on individual countries, cross-national life course research does not have to lead to the impasse of a multitude of unrelated studies of particular life course outcomes and their institutional underpinnings. Both the assumption of a unidirectional effect of highly differentiated institutions and policies and the assumption of meaningful mobility and life course regimes might be possible to salvage.

CONCLUSION

In this chapter I reviewed the current state of comparative, cross-national research on the life course and discussed a number of the substantive and methodological problems faced by this emerging research program. As an initial step I argued how a *differential sociology of the life course* has developed out of more general theories on aging, generations, and human development. Then, I discussed the potential of causally linking institutional features of societies to life course outcomes using either historical or cross-national comparisons. Due to the inherent difficulty of temporally matching periods with stable institutional settings to lives, I concluded that cross-national comparisons are better suited to untangle such linkages. In regard to the latter, several issues have to be tackled: Are single countries or ensembles of countries the appropriate unit of analysis? Are single countries or specific institutional arrangements the proper independent variable? Do institutions form "regimes" or "clusters"? And, finally, do life course outcomes form "regimes" or do they, as dependent variables, have to be considered separately? My answers are straightforward: (1) Aggregating countries into typologies or regimes might be defensible as shortcuts to interpretation but is more misleading than useful in developing and testing hypotheses about causal linkages. (2) Nationally varying institutional arrangements need to be disaggregated and matched to specific life course outcomes. (3) However, both on the side of institutions as bodies of rules and as incentive structures and on the side of life course outcomes, researchers can observe nonrandom, systematic patterns of association. This allows social scientists to retain the idea of *country-specific life course regimes* at least as a fruitful heuristic in further studies. One major objection that might be raised against my assessment is that it neglects institutional changes within countries. Such changes obviously would complicate matters even more, but including them would only strengthen my main argument in favor of within-country specificity.

Notes

1. I gratefully acknowledge the research assistance of Janette Kawachi and the assistance of Helena Maravilla in preparing the manuscript. I am also grateful to Tom DiPrete, Janne Jonsson, Janette Kawachi, Dirk Konietzka, David Soskice, Stefan Svallfors, and the participants of the Sigtuna Symposium in Honor of Robert

Erikson for both encouraging and critical comments. They share no responsibility for the final product.

2. This view might be contested. While education differentials at age of leaving home are smaller than differences in country means, for example, between Italy and Germany (Rusconi 2003), the variance in age at first child is probably bigger within countries than between countries.

3. This assumption has—under the name of path dependency—become quite fashionable and it is often falsely taken to be a self-sufficient explanation.

4. The relationship between life courses (when does what happen?) and social inequality (who gets how much?) is not well developed. The social organization of lives has been postulated as rival socialization and institutional pattern to social stratification (Kohli 1985) or it has been assumed to be one of its major generating mechanisms (Mayer and Carroll 1987). For an argument about why stratification and mobility research needs to be complemented by life course research, see DiPrete 2002.

5. I owe the clarification in this paragraph to Tom DiPrete.

6. At this stage, they should be taken as hypotheses rather than fully tested evidence.

7. I am sidestepping the issue of whether, why, and to which extent institutions form "ensembles" or "regimes." On this question of "institutional complementarities," see Streeck 1997 and Hall and Soskice 2001.

8. Although almost all those eligible take up this incentive to transit from unemployment to early retirement, it did little to reduce unemployment levels.

References

Allmendinger, Jutta. 1989a. *Career Mobility Dynamics: A Comparative Study of the United States, Norway and Germany* (Studien und Berichte Nr. 49). Berlin: Max-Planck-Institut für Bildungsforschung.

Allmendinger, Jutta. 1989b. Educational Systems and Labor Market Outcomes. *European Sociological Review* 5(2):231–250.

Allmendinger, Jutta and Hinz, Thomas. 1998. Occupational Careers Under Different Welfare Regimes: West Germany, Great Britain and Sweden. Pp. 63–84. In Lutz Leisering and Robert Walker (eds.), *The Dynamics of Modern Society: Poverty, Policy and Welfare*. Bristol: Policy Press.

Anderson, Michael. 1985. The Emergence of the Modern Life Cycle in Britain. *Social History* 10(1):69–87.

Aries, Philippe. 1973. *Centuries of Childhood*. Harmondsworth: Penguin.

Bertaux, Daniel (ed.). 1981. *Biography and Society: The Life History Approach in the Social Sciences*. Beverly Hills, Calif.: Sage.

Blau, Francine D. and Kahn, Lawrence M. (eds.). 2002. *At Home and Abroad: U.S. Labor Market Performance in International Perspective*. New York: Russell Sage Foundation.

Blossfeld, Hans-Peter. 2003. Globalisation, Social Inequality and the Role of Coun-try-Specific Institutions. Pp. 303–324. In Pedro Conceição, Manuel V. Heitor, and Bengt-Åke Lundvall (eds.), *Innovation, Competence Building and Social Cohesion in Europe: Towards a Learning Society*. Cheltenham, UK: Edward Elgar.

Blossfeld, Hans-Peter and Drobnic, Sonja (eds.). 2001. *Careers of Couples in Con-temporary Society. From Male Breadwinner to Dual-Earner Families*. Oxford: Oxford University Press.

Blossfeld, Hans-Peter and Hakim, Catherine (eds.). 1997. *Between Equalization and Marginalization. Women Working Part-Time in Europe and the United States of America*. Oxford: Oxford University Press.

Boyer, Robert and Durand, Jean-Pierre (eds.). 1997. *After Fordism*. Hampshire, NY: Palgrave.

Breen, Richard and Buchmann, Marlis. 2002. Institutional Variation and the Posi-tion of Young People: A Comparative Perspective. Pp. 288–305. In Frank F. Furstenberg Jr. (ed.), *Early Adulthood in Cross-National Perspective* (The An-nals of the American Academy of Political and Social Science, vol. 580, March 2002). Thousand Oaks, Calif.: Sage.

Buchmann, Marlis. 1989. *The Script of Life in Modern Society. Entry Into Adult-hood in a Changing World*. Chicago: University of Chicago Press.

Bude, Heinz. 1995. *Das Altern einer Generation. Die Jahrgänge 1938 bis 1948*. Frankfurt am Main: Suhrkamp Verlag.

Clausen, John A. 1986 *The Life Course. A Sociological Perspective*. Englewood Cliffs, N.J.: Prentice Hall.

Crouch, Colin. 2001. Welfare State Regimes and Industrial Relations Systems: The Questionable Role of Path Dependency Theory. Pp. 105–124. In Bern-hard Ebbinghaus and Philip Manow (eds.), *Comparing Welfare Capitalism: Social Policy and Political Economy in Europe, Japan and the USA*. London: Routledge.

Crouch, Colin and Streeck, Wolfgang (eds.). 1997. *Political Economy of Modern Capitalism. Mapping Convergence and Diversity*. London: Sage.

DiPrete, Thomas A. 2002. Life Course Risks, Mobility Regimes, and Mobility Consequences: A Comparison of Sweden, Germany, and the United States. *American Journal of Sociology* 108(2) September 2002:267–309.

DiPrete, Thomas A., Maurin, Eric, Goux, Dominique, and Quesnell-Vallee, Ame-lie. 2003. Work and Pay in Flexible and Regulated Labor Markets: A Gener-alized Perspective on Institutional Evolution and Inequality Trends in Europe and the U.S. Ms. Duke University, Durham, NC.

Ebbinghaus, Bernhard. 2002. Exit from Labor. Reforming Early Retirement and Social Partnership in Europe, Japan, and the USA. Habilitation, Universität zu Köln.

Ebbinghaus, Bernhard, and Manow, Philip (eds.). 2001a. *Comparing Welfare Capitalism. Social policy and political economy in Europe, Japan and the*

USA, (Routledge/EUI Studies in the Political Economy of Welfare). London: Routledge.

Ebbinghaus, Bernhard and Manow, Philip. 2001b. Introduction: Studying Varieties of Welfare Capitalism. Pp. 1–24. In Bernhard Ebbinghaus and Philip Manow (eds.), *Comparing Welfare Capitalism: Social Policy and Political Economy in Europe, Japan and the USA*. London: Routledge.

Eisenstadt, Shmuel N. 1964. *From Generation to Generation: Age Groups and Social Structure*. New York: Free Press of Glencoe.

Elder, Glen H. Jr. 1974. *Children of the Great Depression*. Chicago: University of Chicago Press.

Elder, Glen H. Jr. and Conger, Rand D. (eds.). 2000. *Children of the Land. Adversity and Success in Rural America*. Chicago: University of Chicago Press.

Erikson, Erik H. 1980. *Identity and the Life Cycle*. New York: Norton.

Erikson, Robert and Goldthorpe, John H. 1992. *The Constant Flux: A Study of Class Mobility in Industrial Societies*. Oxford: Clarendon.

Esping-Andersen, Gøsta. 2002. A New Gender Contract. Pp. 68–95. In Gøsta Esping-Andersen (ed.), *Why We Need a Welfare State*. Oxford: Oxford University Press.

Esping-Andersen, Gøsta. 1999. *Social Foundations of Postindustrial Economies*. Oxford: Oxford University Press.

Esping-Andersen, Gøsta. 1990. *The Three Worlds of Welfare Capitalism*. Princeton, N.J.: Princeton University Press.

Hall, Peter A. and Soskice, David (eds.). 2001. *Varieties of Capitalism: The Institutional Foundations of Comparative Advantage*. Oxford: Oxford University Press.

Hareven, Tamara (ed.). 1996. *Aging and Generational Relations: Life Course and Cross-Cultural Perspectives*. New York: Aldine de Gruyter.

Hareven, Tamara. 1986. Historical Changes in the Social Construction of the Life Course. *Human Development* 29(3):171–180.

Held, Thomas. 1986. Institutionalization and Deinstitutionalization of the Life Course. *Human Development* 29(3):157–162.

Hillmert, Steffen. 2001. *Ausbildungssysteme und Arbeitsmarkt. Lebensverläufe in Grossbritannien und Deutschland im Kohortenvergleich*, (Studien zur Sozialwissenschaft, vol. 212). Wiesbaden: Westdeutscher Verlag.

Hoem, Britta. 2000. Entry into Motherhood in Sweden: The Influence of Economic Factors on the Rise and Fall in Fertility, 1986–1997. *Demographic Research* 2(4). http://www.demographic-research.org/volumes/vol2/4

Hoem, Jan M., Prskawetz, Alexia, and Neyer, Gerda. 2001. Autonomy or Conservative Adjustment? The Effect of Public Policies and Educational Attainment on Third Births in Austria, 1975–96 (Reprinted in the Vienna Yearbook of Population Research 2003, 101–119). *Population Studies* 55(3):249–261. http://www.demogr.mpg.de/Papers/Working/wp-2001-016.pdf

Huinink, Johannes. 1995. *Warum noch Familie? Zur Attraktivität von Partner-*

schaft und Elternschaft in unserer Gesellschaft. Frankfurt am Main: Campus Verlag.

Iversen, Torben and Rosenbluth, Frances. 2003. The Political Economy of Gender: Explaining Cross-National Variation in Household Bargaining, Divorce and the Gender Voting Gap. Working Paper. Department of Political Science, Yale University, New Haven. http://www.yale.edu/polisci/rosenbluth/IversenRosenbluth.pdf

Jacob, Marita. 2003. Ausmaß, Struktur und Ursachen von Mehrfachausbildungen. Eine Analyse von Ausbildungsverläufen in den achtziger und neunziger Jahren in Westdeutschland. Dissertation, Institut für Soziologie, Freie Universität, Berlin.

Jonsson, Jan O. and Mills, Colin (eds.), 2001. *Cradle to Grave: Life-course Change in Modern Sweden.* Durham, England: Sociologypress.

Kohli, Martin. 1987. Retirement and the Moral Economy: An Historical Interpretation of the German Case. *Journal of Aging Studies* 1:125–144.

Kohli, Martin. 1985. Die Institutionalisierung des Lebenslaufs. Historische Befunde und theoretische Argumente. *Kölner Zeitschrift für Soziologie und Sozialpsychologie* 37:1–29.

Kohli, Martin. 1981. Biography: Account, Text, Method. Pp. 61–75. In Daniel Bertaux (ed.), *Biography and Society: The Life History Approach in the Social Sciences.* Beverly Hills, Calif.: Sage.

Korpi, Tomas and Mertens, Antje. 2003. Training Systems and Labor Mobility: A Comparison between Germany and Sweden. *The Scandinavian Journal of Economics* 105(4):597–617.

Leisering, Lutz. 2003. Government and the Life Course. Pp. 205–225. In Jeylan T. Martimer and Michael J. Shanahan (eds.), *Handbook of the Life Course.* New York: Kluwer Academic/Plenum.

Leisering, Lutz and Leibfried, Stephan. 1999. *Time and Poverty in the Welfare State: United Germany in Perspective.* Cambridge: Cambridge University Press.

Mannheim, Karl. 1952. The Sociological Problem of Generations. Pp. 276–322. In P. Kecskemeti (ed.), *Essays on the Sociology of Knowledge.* New York: Routledge and Paul.

Mannheim, Karl. 1928. Das Problem der Generationen. *Kölner Vierteljahreshefte für Soziologie* VII. (Reprinted in: Karl Mannheim: Das Problem der Generationen. Pp. 509–565. In Kurt H. Wolff (ed.): *Karl Mannheim: Wissenssoziologie. Auswahl aus dem Werk.* Neuwied/Berlin 1964).

Mayer, Karl Ulrich. 2003. Small Children Should Have Their Mother At Home! Culture, Institutions and Policies Shaping Women's Work-Family-Career Interface in West and East Germany. Paper presented at the 98th Annual Meeting of the American Sociological Association. Atlanta, Ga., August 16–19, 2003.

Mayer, Karl Ulrich. 2001. The Paradox of Global Social Change and National Path Dependencies: Life Course Patterns in Advanced Societies. Pp. 89–110. In Alison E. Woodward and Martin Kohli (eds.), *Inclusions and Exclusions in European Societies*. London: Routledge.

Mayer, Karl Ulrich. 1997. Notes on a Comparative Political Economy of Life Courses. *Comparative Social Research* 16:203–226.

Mayer, Karl Ulrich. 1995. Gesellschaftlicher Wandel, Kohortenungleichheit und Lebensverläufe. Pp. 27–47. In Peter A. Berger and Peter Sopp (eds.), *Sozialstruktur und Lebenslauf*. Opladen: Leske + Budrich.

Mayer, Karl Ulrich. 1994. The Postponed Generation: Economic, Political, Social, and Cultural Determinants of Changes in Life Course Regimes. Pp. 47–69. In Henk A. Becker and Piet L. J. Hermkens (eds.), *Solidarity of Generations: Demographic, Economic and Social Change, and its Consequences*. Amsterdam: Thesis Publishers.

Mayer, Karl Ulrich (ed.). 1990. *Lebensverläufe und sozialer Wandel (Sonderheft 31 der Kölner Zeitschrift für Soziologie und Sozialpsychologie)*. Opladen: Westdeutscher Verlag.

Mayer, Karl Ulrich and Carroll, Glenn R. 1987. Jobs and Classes: Structural Constraints on Career Mobility. *European Sociological Review* 3(1):14–38.

Mayer, Karl Ulrich and Hillmert, Steffen. 2003. New Ways of Life or Old Rigidities? Changes in Social Structures and Life Courses and their Political Impact. Pp. 79–100. In Herbert Kitschelt and Wolfgang Streeck (eds.), *West European Politics* (Special Issue on *Germany: Beyond the Stable State*, vol. 26, Nr. 4, October). London: Frank Cass.

Mayer, Karl Ulrich and Huinink, Johannes. 1993. Lebensverläufe und Gesellschaftlicher Wandel: Von der Kohortenanalyse zur Lebensverlaufsanalyse. Pp. 92–111. In Richard Hauser, Uwe Hochmuth, and Johannes Schwarze (eds.), *Mikroanalytische Grundlagen der Gesellschaftspolitik. (Band 1—Sonderforschungsbereiche)*. Berlin: Akademie Verlag.

Mayer, Karl Ulrich and Müller, Walter. 1986. The State and the Structure of the Life Course. Pp. 217–245. In Aage B. Sørensen, Franz E. Weinert, and Lonnie R. Sherrod (eds.), *Human Development and the Life Course: Multidisciplinary Perspectives*. Hillsdale, N.J.: Lawrence Erlbaum.

Mayer, Karl Ulrich and Schoepflin, Urs. 1989. The State and the Life Course. *Annual Review of Sociology* 15:187–209.

Mills, Melinda and Blossfeld, Hans-Peter. 2003. Globalization, Uncertainty and Changes in Early Life Courses. *Zeitschrift für Erziehungswissenschaft* 6(2):188–219.

Modell, John. 1991. *Into One's Own: From Youth to Adulthood in the United States 1920–1975*. Berkeley: University of California Press.

Modell, John, Furstenberg, Frank F., and Hershberg, Theodore. 1976. Social Change and Transition to Adulthood in Historical Perspective. *Journal of Family History* 1(1):7–32.

Myles, John. 1993. Is There a Post-Fordist Life Course? Pp. 171–185. In Walter R. Heinz (ed.), *Institutions and Gatekeeping in the Life Course*. Weinheim: Deutscher Studien-Verlag.

Oppenheimer, Valerie K. and Kalmijn, Matthijs. 1995. Life Cycle Jobs. *Research in Social Stratification and Mobility* 14:1–38.

Parsons, Talcott. 1942. Age and Sex in the Social Structure of the United States. *American Sociological Review* 7:604–616.

Pettit, Becky and Western, Bruce. 2004. Mass Imprisonment and the Life Course: Race and Class Inequality in U.S. Incarceration. *American Sociological Review* 69 (2):151–169.

Riley, Matilda White, Kahn, Robert L., and Foner, Anne (eds.). 1994. *Age and Structural Lag: Society's Failure to Provide Meaningful Opportunities in Work, Family, and Leisure*. New York: John Wiley & Sons.

Rosenbluth, Frances. 2000. The Comparative Political Economy of Childcare: Japan, U.S., and Europe. Working Paper. Department of Political Science, Yale University, New Haven. http://pantheon.yale.edu/rosenblu/Childcar.htm

Rosenbluth, Frances, Light, Matthew, and Schrag, Claudia. 2002. The Politics of Low Fertility: Global Markets, Women's Employment, and Birth Rates in Four Industrialized Democracies. Working Paper. Department of Political Science, Yale University, New Haven. http://www.yale.edu/polisci/rosenbluth/politics%20of%20Low%20Fertility%201.htm

Rowntree, Benjamin Seebohm. 1914. *Poverty. A Study in Town Life*. London: Nelson (first published 1901).

Rusconi, Alessandra. 2003. Leaving the Parental Home in Italy and West Germany: Opportunities and Constraints. Dissertation, Fachbereich Politik- und Sozialwissenschaften, Freie Universität, Berlin.

Ryder, Norman B. 1980. *The Cohort Approach. Essays in the Measurement of Temporal Variations in Demographic Behavior*. New York: Arno.

Ryder, Norman B. 1965. The Cohort as a Concept in the Study of Social Change. *American Sociological Review* 30:843–861.

Scharpf, Fritz W. and Schmidt, Vivien A. (eds.). 2000a. *Welfare and Work in the Open Economy. From Vulnerability to Competitiveness*, vol. 1. Oxford: Oxford University Press.

Scharpf, Fritz W. and Schmidt Vivien A. (eds.). 2000b. *Welfare and Work in the Open Economy. Diverse Responses to Common Challenges*, vol. 2. Oxford: Oxford University Press.

Solga, Heike. 2003. Ohne Abschluss in die Bildungsgesellschaft. Die Erwerbschancen gering qualifizierter Personen aus soziologischer und ökonomischer Perspektive. Habilitation, Institut für Soziologie, Freie Universität, Berlin.

Sørensen, Aage B. 1990. Processes of Allocation to Open and Closed Positions in Social Structure. Pp. 256–287. In Joseph Berger and Morris Zelditch Jr. (eds.), *Sociological Theories in Progress*, vol. 3. New York: Sage.

Sørensen, Aage B. 1986. Theory and Methodology in Social Stratification. Pp. 69–

95. In Ulf Himmelstrand (ed.), *The Sociology of Structure and Action*. New York: Sage.

Soskice, David. 1991. The Institutional Infrastructure for International Competitiveness: A Comparative Analysis of the UK and Germany. Pp. 45–66. In A. B. Atkinson and Renato Brunetta (eds.), *Economics of the New Europe*. London: Macmillan.

Stinchcombe, Arthur Leonard. 1987. *Constructing Social Theories*. Chicago: University of Chicago Press.

Streeck, Wolfgang. 1997. Beneficial Constraints: On the Economic Limits of Rational Voluntarism. Pp. 197–219. In J. Rogers Hollingsworth and Robert Boyer (eds.), *Contemporary Capitalism: The Embeddedness of Institutions*. Cambridge: Cambridge University Press.

Thomas, William I. and Znaniecki, Florian. 1918. *The Polish Peasant in Europe and in America. Monograph of an Immigrant Group*. Chicago: University of Chicago Press.

CHAPTER THREE

Progress in Sociology:
The Case of Social Mobility Research

John H. Goldthorpe

The issue I start from is that of whether sociology progresses. Is it possible to demonstrate a cumulative growth in sociological knowledge and understanding? Of late, sociologists themselves have often given negative, or at best uncertain, answers to this question.

Some, for example, believe that it is mistaken in principle to expect progress in sociology. An extreme, postmodernist view is that scientific progress is in general an illusion; all knowledge is in fact locally conditioned and, thus, relative. But a somewhat more plausible claim is that while progress can, and does, occur in the natural sciences, the social sciences are a quite different kind of undertaking in which the possibility of progress is far more doubtful, and especially as regards theoretical knowledge.

Thus, authors such as Bryant (1995: 4–6) and Flyvbjerg (2001: 25–37) have contended that all attempts in sociology to develop "theory proper"— that is, theory in the sense of the natural sciences that aims at steadily growing explanatory power across a range of empirically established phenomena—are doomed to failure. For these authors, the underlying problem is ontological in character. In Bryant's words, for theory proper to be possible in sociology, human societies would "have to be constituted differently from the way they are" (1995: 6). The argument sustaining this position is not easily followed. It starts from the observation that while the natural sciences deal with physical entities, the social sciences are concerned with "self-reflecting humans" (Flyvbjerg, 2001: 32) who "construct" their own social world. On this basis, two further claims are then made—with, so far as I can see, no very adequate logical or empirical backing: first, that since sociologists are part of the "reality" they study, their concepts necessarily depend on, and are in constant interaction with, those that are embedded in the everyday lives of lay actors; and, second, that all propositions made by sociologists that aim at generality will thus be rendered inherently unstable, because such propositions will in fact need to change in response to changes in lay actors' own understandings and interpretations of their social worlds— and including those that are prompted by the practice of sociology itself.[1]

However, despite the unsatisfactory nature of the argument, the conclusion to which it supposedly leads is clear enough. Sociology has to be an essentially hermeneutic discipline whose practitioners, like lay members of society themselves, can aim only at interpretation, not explanation, of the social world, and thus at producing not science, at least on anything like the natural science model, but rather discourse of, perhaps, some moral and pragmatic significance.[2]

Another group of authors can be identified who are less concerned with a priori arguments than with the apparent *fact* that progress in sociology has, so far at least, not matched that achieved in the natural sciences. Thus, Cole (1994; cf. also 1992) maintains that although in sociology and the natural sciences alike disputes about what counts as knowledge are quite common on the "periphery"—where science is, as it were, in the making—sociology is then far less successful than the natural sciences in the transfer of knowledge from the periphery to the "core": that is, to a growing body of knowledge that is generally accepted as valid and important. Cole sees two main difficulties facing sociology in this regard. The first is again one that relates to the phenomena with which sociology deals: whether or not because of fundamental ontological differences, these phenomena are more *mutable*, over time and space, history and culture, than those dealt with by the natural sciences. The second difficulty is that sociologists, in choosing the problems they study, are far more likely than natural scientists to be influenced by personal interests, values, and ideologies than by purely cognitive considerations, including that of how do-able a particular research project is.

Rule (1997) takes up similar questions to Cole but focuses on the way in which sociological theory, rather than developing systematically, both prompted and constrained by research, tends more to follow intellectual taste and fashion. In sociology, building on what went before does not carry the same kudos as being à la mode. In the end, though, Rule is somewhat more optimistic than Cole. "Theory for coping"—that is, theory that tries to provide some understanding of how societies objectively form and constrain the experience of their members—shows, he believes, more evidence of progress than "theory as expression," which seems chiefly to be a reflection of the experiential reality of those individuals who produce it.

In what follows, I address issues of the kind raised by the authors I have referred to, though taking the second group a good deal more seriously than the first. My argument is therefore far more empirical than philosophical or methodological in character and, moreover, relates to just one area of sociological work: that is, the study of social mobility. My purpose will be to show that in this case, at least, progress in sociology can, in some meaningful sense, be documented—which is in itself enough to undermine the more extreme "impossibilist" position, without need to enter further into its obscure foundations. I accept that important differences exist between the natural and the social sciences, broadly on the lines indicated by Cole. But these I take as being differences of degree, and not of kind, that do not require or justify any kind of intellectual apartheid. I also accept that what may be true of social mobility research need not—indeed does not—hold good for other areas of sociology, and thus, in conclusion, I make some suggestions as to why this might be so.

I am, I should add, uncomfortably aware that because social mobility is the field in which a large part of my own research has been carried out, it might well appear that in arguing for progress in this field, I am attempting to create glory in the reflection of which I can then myself bask. By way of offsetting this possibility, I would therefore emphasize—and consistently with my general theme—a distinctive feature of achievement in science, as distinct, say, from in the arts: that is, that while scientific achievement may be associated with the names of particular individuals, it is in a more fundamental sense *collective* in character. The best indication of this is that if any truly scientific achievement had not been made by X or Y, then, sooner or later, it would have been made by Z—in contrast to an achievement such as, say, *Hamlet*, which, if it had not been written by Shakespeare, would not have been written at all (cf. Wolpert 1992). In so far, then, as I am correct in holding that, in social mobility research, sociology can show something recognizable as scientific progress, all individual contributions will need to be understood as grounded in, and as expressions of, an enterprise in which many others were integrally involved.

PROGRESS IN SOCIAL MOBILITY RESEARCH

Discussion of the possibility or actuality of progress in sociology has tended to center on theory. However, although a special importance may indeed attach to theory, questions of progress in other respects need not, and should not, be neglected. I therefore consider progress in social mobility research under the heads of data, concepts and analysis, and empirical findings before coming to theory. In no case, I must stress, do I try to provide anything like a comprehensive account of developments over the half-century or more in which the study of social mobility has formed an identifiable specialty within sociology; nor do I focus on the leading edge concerns of the present day. I concentrate, rather, on what seem to me to be the clearest instances of progress in the sense of developments leading to the growth of "core" knowledge in Cole's sense.

Data

An examination of the first general treatise on social mobility, that of Sorokin (1927/1959), shows that the data on which the Sorokin was able to draw were both limited and at the same time highly heterogeneous. The data consisted for the most part of the assessments of historians of rates and patterns of different forms of mobility in various societies of the past—usually based on quite fragmentary sources—supplemented by a miscellany of more contemporary studies, most often ones concerned with what would now be called "elite recruitment": that is, studies of mobility *into* such fairly restricted social groups as millionaires, industrialists, political leaders, and "men of genius."

Taking this situation as baseline, it would then seem evident enough that very substantial progress as regards data has been made, and on two main fronts: *coverage* and *quality*.

In the case of coverage, the key developments could be listed as follows.

1. The growing availability, at least across economically more advanced societies, of data on social mobility derived from surveys representative of national populations. The pioneering study here was that directed by Glass (1954) in Great Britain in 1947, which produced a wide range of information relevant to the intergenerational mobility of adult men and women and also detailed family and employment histories.[3]

2. The replication over time of such nationally based mobility studies

or the collection of data relevant to mobility in relatively frequent general-purpose national surveys. In this way, substantial datasets of repeated cross-sectional format have been built up, some now extending over three or four decades, that provide a sound basis for establishing societal trends in mobility.

3. The supplementation of data on mobility from one-off or repeated cross-sectional inquiries (and from retrospective life history studies) by data from prospective panel or birth cohort studies. Such studies allow an alternative perspective on mobility trends and also provide the most appropriate kind of data for testing theories of the causal processes that underlie mobility rates and patterns.

In the case of data quality, the following advances could be singled out.

1. Improvements in the coding of data relevant to mobility, in particular occupational and educational data. In Glass's study, for example, occupational data were "category" coded to the very informally constructed Hall-Jones prestige scale—with demonstrably low reliability. In later studies, the "index" coding of occupational data to relatively well-specified scales or classifications has become standard.

2. Tests of the accuracy of information reported in interviews and of the overall degree of reliability of data, taking into account both recall and recording as well as coding error. Such tests, although giving generally satisfactory results, have also identified instances where reliability is likely to be lowest—for example, respondents' reports on their own, or their parents', occupations in the fairly distant past (cf. Hope et al. 1986; Breen and Jonsson 1997).

3. Improvements in the comparability of data used in cross-national studies of mobility. In early studies of this kind in the tradition of Lipset and Zetterberg (1956), comparability was sought, though not very successfully, simply through the collapsing of the coding categories used in different national inquiries to some lowest common denominator. In later work, however, occupational scales specifically devised for cross-national research (e.g., Treiman 1977; Ganzeboom and Treiman 1996) have been used; or original data have been re-coded to widely applicable—and by now widely employed—classifications, notably the CASMIN class schema (Erikson and Goldthorpe 1992) and the CASMIN educational classification (König et al. 1988; Brauns and Steinmann 1999).

Those who believe that nothing recognizable as scientific progress occurs, or should indeed be expected to occur, in sociology would probably regard advances of the kind noted above as being "merely technical" in character and of little intellectual significance. But such a view would reveal a rather basic misunderstanding of science and, in particular, of the way in which, as the history of the natural sciences well illustrates, progress in fact often directly depends on developments in observational methods that allow new and better data to be produced. The maxim that "New instruments make new science" is well founded (Crump 2002). Moreover, as Steuer (2002) has argued, one of ways in which the social sciences could be thought to differ—in degree—from the natural sciences is that, partly on account of the greater mutability of the phenomena with which they deal, they tend to call for a "more painstaking and ingenious uncovering of the facts" (p. 405). Thus, for the social sciences, improvements in techniques of data collection often represent a distinctive challenge and, insofar as they are brought about, an achievement of corresponding importance.

Concepts and Analysis

In social mobility research the question of the *conceptual context* within which mobility should be studied has from the first received a good deal of attention. Should mobility be defined, observed, and measured in terms of, say, a hierarchy of occupational prestige or socioeconomic status or, alternatively, of positions identified within an occupational or class structure (cf. Glass 1954 and Svalastoga 1959 with Carlsson 1958).

However, it is not in the resolution of conceptual issues of this kind that progress is to be looked for—that is in the sense of a steady movement toward "the one best way." In fact, although divisions remain among researchers about which approach is, overall, the most revealing, there is by now fairly wide agreement, first, that different approaches are more or less appropriate to different problems; and, second, that the empirical findings that emerge within alternative conceptual contexts differ in their detail rather than in their more salient and consequential features.[4] In other words, a clear indication is here provided that concepts and their provenance are less crucial in constructing sociological knowledge than those who deny the possibility of a scientific sociology would seem to suppose, and that more important are the *propositions* to which concepts, as applied in research, actually give rise (cf. Popper 1976: 21–28 esp.; 1994: ch. 2.).

Where conceptual progress may properly be sought, and indeed found, in mobility research is where it is associated with the solution of specific analytical problems, and ones that arise however the context of mobility may be understood. In this regard, progress can most readily be seen in the analysis of intergenerational mobility (or, more generally, of mobility envisaged as transitions between "origins" and "destinations" rather than in a complete life course perspective).[5]

In the work of Glass and others of his generation, the main basis for the analysis of mobility was a contingency table—now known as the standard mobility table—in which individuals' origins, as categorized according to status or class, were crossed with their destinations, categorized in a similar way. Analysis then consisted of various operations performed on counts in the internal and marginal cells of the table. In such analysis, two major problems arose, in dealing with each of which later researchers can claim to have achieved genuine advances in "ways of thinking" about social mobility.

1. While the standard mobility table provided an appropriate basis for the calculation of percentage outflow and inflow rates of mobility, it was not easy to adapt it so as to bring into the analysis factors of likely importance in mediating mobility—for example, education. Progress in this respect, was, however, made, chiefly under the leadership of Duncan (Duncan and Hodge 1963; Blau and Duncan 1967), through the adoption of a regression approach. Destination became the dependent variable, while origin was an independent explanatory variable taken together with education and whatever other intervening variables might be deemed of interest. Moreover, in so far as these latter variables could be placed in some likely temporal sequence, path-analytic techniques could be used in order to "decompose" the gross correlation of origins and destinations into a direct and a series of indirect effects. In this way, then, the resolution of a technical difficulty went together with a fairly radical conceptual reorientation. The relationship between origins and destinations was no longer treated simply in terms of mobility but was rather seen as the outcome of a *process* of status attainment (because Duncan and his associates worked chiefly with a scoring or ranking of occupations on a socioeconomic status scale).

2. The standard mobility table also served as a basis for efforts to separate out the effects on observed (e.g., percentage) mobility rates of, on the one hand, differences between the two marginal distributions of the table (seen as the source of "structural" mobility) and, on the other, the pattern of net association prevailing between origins and destinations (seen as the source of "exchange" mobility). However, efforts in this direction remained unsatisfactory until a new approach via loglinear modeling was introduced by Hauser (Hauser et al. 1975; Hauser 1978). This modeling allowed patterns of origin-destination association within the mobility table to be analyzed in a "margin-insensitive" way; and, at the same time, it led to a progressive shift away from the old idea of total mobility being made up of structural and exchange com-

ponents to the more viable and revealing distinction between absolute and relative mobility rates (Goldthorpe 1980/1987; Erikson and Goldthorpe 1992).

The two developments noted above had certain divergent aspects. The status attainment approach, although facilitating multivariate analysis, was most readily implemented with continuous variables—such as status scores, years of education—and by making the (heroic) assumption of linear and additive effects. In contrast, loglinear modeling, while remaining largely bivariate, made possible detailed analyses of mobility tables, organized on the basis of class or occupational categories, through which "endogenous mobility regimes," could be identified: that is, persisting patterns of relative rates or, alternatively, varying levels of (net) association for different origin-destination transitions.

However, in recent years further progress has been made in integrating these two approaches and combining their strengths. Most importantly, the possibility has been developed (Logan 1983; Breen 1994) of reformulating loglinear models for the grouped data of standard mobility tables as multinomial logistic regression models for individual-level data, in which a range of other variables, whether categorical or continuous, can be included. Analyses that follow this strategy (e.g. Hendrickx and Ganzeboom 1998; Breen and Goldthorpe 1999, 2001) are in fact now producing new empirical findings, especially in regard to the role of education in mobility processes, that have in turn important theoretical implications, as will be seen in the sections to follow.[6]

Again, then, the advances here reviewed cannot be dismissed as of only technical interest. What is indicated is that it is in grappling with, and solving, technical problems, rather than through *lucubrations de chambre*, that conceptual advances of real consequence are most likely to be made. To claim that the possibility of progress in sociology is compromised by the dependence of its concepts on those of lay members of society is in fact to overlook the capacity of working sociologists to form concepts of their own that are distinct from those of lay members and that, as the next section in particular shows, are crucially involved in the growth of knowledge of a kind that lay members, in the course of their everyday lives, have little need, as well as little opportunity, to acquire.

Empirical Findings

In this regard, progress is best demonstrated by the establishment, in an in-creasingly refined form, of a series of empirical regularities that extend across a relatively wide range of institutional and cultural contexts. Such progress has been most marked in the study of intergenerational mobility—again as in the case of conceptual and analytical developments—and has in-deed occurred in close conjunction with the latter. Of the findings in ques-tion, the following could be reckoned most important.

1. Endogenous mobility regimes—or patterns of relative mobility rates—show a high degree of temporal stability within national societies, often re-maining only little changed over many decades (Erikson and Goldthorpe 1992; Wong 1994). Statistical models postulating constant relative rates over such time periods typically misclassify less than 5 percent of all cases in standard mobility tables. The change that does occur is mostly nondirectional in char-acter—that is, not uniformly toward more or less equal relative rates—but, where it is directional, it is more often toward more equal relative rates or, that is, toward increased rather than decreased fluidity (Erikson and Gold-thorpe 1992; Breen 2004). However, in most national societies in which there occur such increases in fluidity turn out to be limited to a particular period or birth cohort rather than being continuous.[7]

2. Endogenous mobility regimes also show a notable degree of cross-national commonality, at least so far as the overall pattern of relative rates is concerned (Featherman et al. 1975; Grusky and Hauser 1984; Erikson and Goldthorpe 1992: chs. 4 and 5). And, further, claims of national "exceptional-ism" as regards distinctively high (or low) levels of social fluidity or openness find little support. At the same time, the significant cross-national differences in endogenous mobility regimes that do exist can be more readily related to nationally specific institutional or cultural factors or historical circumstances than to more general societal processes, such as industrialization or modern-ization, or to types of political regime (Erikson 1990; Wong 1990; Erikson and Goldthorpe 1992; Rijken 1999).[8]

3. As a corollary of (1) and (2), variation in absolute mobility rates, which is often substantial both over time and cross-nationally, has to be attributed overwhelmingly to structural effects: that is, to shifts in the distributions of populations over the levels of status or the occupational groups or classes in relation to which mobility is defined.

4. In all modern societies, the most important factor mediating intergener-ational mobility is individuals' educational attainment; other relevant individ-ual characteristics, such as IQ or motivation, appear to operate to a large ex-tent via educational attainment. However, no society has yet become a true

meritocracy in the sense that individuals' social origins and destinations are statistically independent once education—or IQ, motivation, or other merit variables—are controlled: a direct effect of origins persists (Marshall et al. 1997; Breen and Goldthorpe 1999, 2001). Moreover, the importance of education in mediating mobility does not steadily increase over time. On the one hand, the association between origins and educational attainment (controlling for the direct effects of educational expansion) weakens, if at all, only slowly (Blossfeld and Shavit 1993); and, on the other hand, several recent national studies indicate that the association between education and destinations is itself now showing a tendency to weaken rather than to strengthen (see Breen 2004).

5. In the associations between origins, education, and destinations, a significant interaction effect is regularly present (contrary to the assumption of linear and additive effects in standard path-analytic models). The association between origins and destinations tends to be weaker at higher educational levels than at lower (Hout 1988; Breen and Jonsson 2003; Vallet 2004); or, in an alternative interpretation, the association between educational attainment and destinations tends to be weaker for individuals of more advantaged origins (Guzzo 2002; cf. also Ishida et al. 1995).

To repeat, what is represented here is a set of fairly well-established empirical regularities—not the expression of iron laws of social mobility. Though in fact extensive, these regularities can then be expected to have their temporal and spatial limits. However, in the present context, two further features of the findings in question call for emphasis.

First, these findings cannot be regarded as obvious or only to be expected, either in their already demonstrated range of applicability or in their actual substance. Indeed, they have in many respects been found surprising, even implausible—contrary to the claim of Giddens (1987: 19–21; 70–1), as invoked by the impossibilists, that because all sociology must be "parasitic" on lay concepts, its findings are always likely to appear "banal." For sociologists, a clear theoretical—that is, explanatory—challenge is then posed.

Second, far from these findings in some way deriving from the lay sociology of the members of the societies to which they relate, these findings are ones that could not conceivably have been arrived at *other than through* the specific procedures of sociologists studying social mobility. That is to say, what they *are* entirely dependent on are developments in techniques of data collection and in concepts and analysis of the kinds that I have previously noted.[9]

Theory

As I earlier observed, discussion of the possibility of progress in sociology has centered on theory. While this appears unduly restrictive and, at least in the case of mobility research, would lead to the quite unjustifiable neglect of progress in other respects, it is clear that the question of whether theoretical advance can be achieved in sociology is one of particular importance.

Early mobility research has to be seen as oriented far more to sociopolitical than to theoretical concerns. After Sorokin's somewhat ad hoc efforts at synthesis, it was not in fact until the 1960s that any further attempt was made to bring empirical findings under the aegis of a theoretical position. However, this attempt was then a highly significant one. Social mobility became one of the main topics in relation to which the currently dominant form of sociological theory—macrosociological functionalism—was actually applied. Suggestive but relatively brief passages in the work of leading proponents of such theory, notably Parsons (e.g., 1960), were taken up and developed both by authors concerned with the analysis of industrial and postindustrial societies, such as Kerr and his associates (1960/1973) and Bell (1973, 1980), and also by a number of specialist mobility researchers, most importantly Blau and Duncan (1967) and Treiman (1970).

Basic to the functionalist theory were the supposed exigencies of modern social systems and in particular, so far as social mobility was concerned, the requirement for human potentialities or resources to be exploited as fully as possible wherever within the social structure they might happen to be located. This requirement was seen as prompting, on the one hand, the progressive expansion and reform of educational institutions in the interests of a greater equality of educational opportunity; and, on the other, the growing importance of educational qualifications as the basis for selection in employment. In turn, as principles of achievement or universalism thus superseded those of ascription or particularism, mobility regimes would be transformed: the association between social origins and destinations would steadily weaken. Or, as Bell (1973: 30) would have it, modern societies were destined in their functional "logic" to become, convergently, education-based meritocracies characterized by their "openness" and rising levels of social fluidity.

This attempt to show functionalist theory actually at work had much to commend it. It clearly brought out the basic form that functionalist explanations take; it provided a reasonable basis for understanding the findings of mobility research up to, say, the end of the 1960s; and, above all, it led to a series of propositions that were eminently open to test in subsequent research. In the 1970s functionalism in general lost its dominance, largely as a result of shifts in ideology and intellectual fashion (thus well illustrating both Cole's and Rule's arguments earlier noted). However, its specific application in the case of social mobility was in fact chiefly undermined by the accumulation of empirical findings that were scarcely consistent with it. As indicated above, both the dependence of educational attainment on social origins and endogenous mobility regimes in themselves have shown a marked resistance to change; and no universal and consistent tendency toward greater social fluidity has been revealed across societies as their industrialization or modernization proceeds.[10] Furthermore, even in those national cases where an increase in openness can be demonstrated, there is often additional evidence—for example, of little if any increase in the role of education in mediating mobility—that points to other causal factors being at work than those that the functionalist theory would propose (see for example on France, Vallet 2004; and on Sweden, Jonsson 2004).

In recent years, therefore, new theoretical efforts have been made that, in contrast to those of the 1960s, are directed as much toward explaining continuity as change in mobility rates and patterns and in the social processes that underlie them. Moreover, as well as being more relevantly oriented toward the main body of empirical findings, these efforts can be seen as progressive in at least two further respects.

    1. While functionalist theory sought a macro-to-macro explanation of mobility rates and patterns in terms of the exigencies of social systems, the aim is now at micro-to-macro explanation in terms of the aggregate outcomes, intended or unintended, of the intended, purposive, or planful actions of individuals (cf. Coleman 1990: ch. 1). The application of functionalist theory to the case of social mobility clearly exposed its lack of adequate microfoundations, as reflected in particular in its inability to explain just why changes *should* come about on the lines needed to meet system exigencies.[11] The new approach, starting from individual action and the idea of "choice under constraint," has so far been chiefly directed toward explanations of persisting differentials in educational attainment, following Boudon's (1974) seminal distinction between primary and secondary processes of educational stratification (e.g., Breen and Goldthorpe 1997; Breen 2001; Jonsson and Erikson 2000; Hillmert and Jacob 2003).[12] However, extensions of this approach have been

made to the explanation of mobility rates and patterns themselves in terms of the "mobility strategies" of individuals and families (Goldthorpe 2000); and, also in this connection, attention is now being given to the hitherto neglected role of employers and their strategies of recruitment and promotion (Jackson et al. 2005).

2. The theory of action that underlies the new approach is of a fairly explicit kind, namely, rational action theory in one form or another, ranging from standard microeconomic theory to versions embodying less extreme, more bounded, conceptions of rationality. In this way, any resort to shifting, ad hoc assumptions is discouraged and, more substantively, the possibility, at least, is created of arriving at more final explanations than those that can be reached via theories of action that end simply with "black-box" appeals to differences in (sub)cultural values or social norms—that is, that do not seek to explain either the specific content of values and norms or the compliance of individuals with them (cf. Boudon 1998, 2003). At the same time, explanatory efforts grounded in rational action theory preserve the merit of functionalist explanations in being open to test, and attempts at the empirical assessment of those noted above are now being made (e.g., Schizzerotto 1997; Davies et al. 2002; Becker 2003; Breen and Yaish 2006) with, so far, reasonably encouraging results.

In both these ways, I would then hold, an advance has been made at least in the *form* of the theory that is applied in mobility research. And the promise that follows of better explanations for the main empirical regularities calling for explanation is already in some part being realized.

In the light of arguments of the kind I noted at the start, such a claim of theoretical progress would seem most likely to be challenged in regard to issues of generality. Authors such as Bryant and Flyvbjerg would, presumably, wish to argue that even if sociologists may rely on their own concepts in establishing *explananda*, any explanation that is grounded in a theory of action must involve some representation of actors' concepts—of *their* understandings and interpretations of the situations in which they act—that must in turn expose sociologists' explanations to instability: that is, make them subject to change as actors' understandings and interpretations change (and, perhaps, in response to sociologists' previous accounts). Consequently, contextual specificity must prevail over generality. Likewise, if more moderately, Cole might maintain that even if *explananda* in the form of empirical regularities extensive in time and space can be determined, these will still have *some* institutional and cultural limits, and so too, therefore, will the generative processes to which explanations of these regularities refer; further, what appear to be the same phenomena may in any case prove to be generated in different ways where different institutional and cultural conditions hold.

My reply to such objections would comprise two, related, points. First, it is possible to accept, as I would, that, in principle, general theory in sociology is always likely to be problematic—chiefly for reasons given by Cole—while, however, still insisting that it is what happens *in practice* that really matters. In other words, the crucial questions are those of *how far* empirical regularities can in fact be established that extend across a range of different societal contexts and of *how far* explanations of these regularities, of some consistent theoretical provenance, can be advanced and stand up to test. It is by reference to considerations such as these that my claim of theoretical progress in social mobility research is made. Ultimately, all theory in sociology may have to be "middle range." Nonetheless, and as Cole does indeed appear to recognize (1994: 152), middle-range theory is still theory. Furthermore, middle range is a matter of degree, and one obvious way in which theories at this level might progress is precisely through their integration and the development of their domains of application.[13]

Second, such a position can be adopted without implying any decisive methodological discontinuity between sociology as a social science and the natural sciences. Those who are most concerned to assert such a discontinuity tend to operate with a restricted and indeed quite old-fashioned idea of the form that theoretical explanation takes in the natural sciences. This they see as explanation that operates by subsuming phenomena under "covering laws" of a universal and deterministic kind—the success of which is indicated by the possibility of prediction. Because in sociology such (successful) covering laws are rare or nonexistent, it is then taken to follow that sociology cannot aim to be scientific.[14] However, it has for some time been recognized that explanation in the natural sciences does not always conform to the covering law model. Often, and especially in the biological sciences, explanation is concerned, rather, with determining causal processes or mechanisms operating at deeper levels than that at which the phenomena of interest are observed (cf. Cox 1992)—on, in fact, essentially similar lines to those noted above in the search for micro-level explanations for regularities in mobility rates and patterns. Although in the natural sciences such causal processes are typically established with much greater theoretical coherence and cogency than, so far at least, in sociology, it is still the case that successful explanation in this mode may not allow for prediction (as, say, in evolutionary biology) or that, because of the mutability of phenomena, may never achieve complete generality (as, say, in ecology). Again, then, the point to be stressed is that the differences that arise between—at least some of—the natural sciences and sociology are ones of degree that in no way warrant qualitative distinctions.[15]

WHY HAS SOCIAL MOBILITY RESEARCH MADE PROGRESS?

On the basis of the foregoing, I would then wish to maintain that in social mobility research over the last half-century or more recognizable progress *has* been made across a wide front—and that the impossibilist position is thus undermined. More and better data have been assembled; ways of conceptualizing and analyzing mobility rates, patterns, and process have steadily improved; empirical knowledge has increased, including knowledge of a growing number of hitherto unsuspected and wide-ranging regularities; and the theoretical task of providing explanations of these regularities is now being taken up in more promising, and already to some extent more productive, ways than before.

To be sure, there are in social mobility research, as in any other field of inquiry, many unresolved problems, areas of uncertainty if not confusion, and issues of contention. But this, I would argue, applies chiefly—to return to Cole's distinction—to the periphery, to the situation on the research frontier, while, contrary to Cole's expectation for sociology at large, a body of generally accepted core knowledge has in fact been established. The strongest support for this claim is found in several surveys of the field written over the recent past by individuals whose positions on the periphery are by no means identical (e.g., Kurz and Müller 1987; Ganzeboom et al. 1991; Treiman and Ganzeboom 2000; Hout and DiPrete 2004). Not surprisingly, these surveys reveal frequent, and sometimes quite sharp, differences of view. However, these mostly concern questions that are accepted as being still open, and that in fact make sense only in the context of a broader consensus that also clearly emerges—and within which, I believe, my own assessment of progress in the field would fall.

As I remarked at the outset, I would not wish to argue that the situation that exists in social mobility research is general throughout sociology. To the contrary, I suspect that for many other fields the case for progress would be far more difficult to make; and, in particular, that Cole's point about the limited transfer of knowledge from periphery to core would prove much harder to deny. This being so, I conclude with some thoughts on the conditions that may have specially favored social mobility research.

First of all, a feature of the institutional context of such research should be noted. Although actually carried out in many different kinds of national institutions, ranging from university departments to central statistical bureaus, social mobility research has, virtually from its origins, been significantly—and, I would think, uniquely—influenced by international exchanges and collaboration, chiefly under the aegis the Research Committee on Social Stratification and Mobility (RC28) of the International Sociological Association. RC28 was founded in 1951 and has been in continuous existence ever since apart from one short hiatus (1969–71). From the 1970s, it has regularly convened on a twice-yearly basis with a membership that comprises a very high proportion of all sociologists who are active in the field.

On the basis of RC28, a research tradition has been created, now extending over several generations, through which a relatively large collectivity of sociologists has given its attention to a set of fairly well defined problems *in a sustained manner.* Again, there are few, if any, parallel cases. Sociologists have not in general been very good at sticking with problems, largely, it seems, because of their undue susceptibility to both ideology and intellectual fashion, which authors such as Cole and Rule rightly see as inimical to cognitive advance. Critics of social mobility research (e.g., Miller 1998) have contended that its concerns have been too narrowly focused. But these critics overlook the possibility that, especially given sociology's still rather modest resources, human and material, there may well be great advantage in any field of research in concentrating these resources on the treatment of a limited number of central problems, and then on working out systematically from these (cf. Treiman and Ganzeboom 2000), rather than adopting a spreadshot approach that could be excessively responsive to transient, noncognitive influences.

It is, moreover, the international character of the collective effort of RC28 that has itself helped to protect the possibility of progress against the distractions of ideology and fashion. The range of ideological positions represented within the committee has always been wide. Most notably, from the early 1970s to the breakup of the Soviet bloc sociologists from this region played a prominent role in its work, and it was therefore a condition of the committee's viability that members should be ready to distinguish between ideological and scientific issues and to find ways of discussing the latter that were acceptable, and profitable, across the ideological spectrum. Their success in this regard is indicated by the committee's long-term survival, although some self-deselection did no doubt occur in the case of those who were committed to positions that would not allow the problem of ideology to be thus "neutralized."

The international composition of RC28 also diffused the impact of fashion on mobility research. What is in sociological vogue at any one time tends to vary a good deal across national societies or geographical regions. Thus, in an international context, what might be represented from any one quarter as the dernier cri is always likely to meet with skepticism from others, and bandwagon effects are inhibited. RC28 has in fact remained remarkably free from the influence of the successive waves of intellectual fashion—from, say, structuralist Marxism, via radical feminism to postmodernism—that have washed over much of sociology. In turn, and more positively, what might be called an international style of sociology has been encouraged that is capable of transcending more local, and passing, enthusiasms.

Finally, in consequence of the above and also of a strong emphasis on methodological issues, social mobility research in the tradition established within RC28 has been characterized by a more serious concern with the actual "do-ability" of projects than has prevailed in many other areas of sociology. Criticism of the narrowness of the interests of mobility researchers of the kind previously noted has typically gone together with criticism of their preoccupation with (primarily quantitative) methods. It is held that methods too often determine research problems rather than the other way around. However, critics again fail to see the other side of the argument: that it is easy to set out ambitious, far-reaching programs for sociological research—but at the same time rather pointless unless the means are available for accomplishing them. As Peter Medawar once aptly observed (1958: 2–3): "If politics is the art of the possible, research is surely the art of the soluble. Both are immensely practical-minded affairs . . . The spectacle of a scientist locked in combat with the forces of ignorance is not an inspiring one if, in the outcome, the scientist is routed." Such a spectacle is, unfortunately, all too familiar in sociology; and social mobility researchers' emphasis on methods reflects the fact that, in their tradition, it is performance not program that matters. If this means that their achievements have indeed been limited rather than over-arching, they have still been achievements. And for those not totally bewitched by *discontinuiste* versions of the history of science, it is still the case that progress is made in small steps as well, perhaps, as through revolutionary paradigm shifts.[16]

Since I remain disturbed by the possibility that this chapter might be regarded simply as a piece of trumpet blowing, the conclusion to which the foregoing points is then somewhat reassuring. I earlier argued that scientific progress has in general to be understood as falling to the credit of individuals only in the rather special sense of individuals operating as the—in large part substitutable—agents of a collectivity. On the more specific issue of progress in sociology, I would now want to add that if this is more apparent in social mobility research than elsewhere, this is not, of course, because social mobility researchers are more able, or in any other sense more worthy, than sociologists working in other fields but rather because of the way in which, as a collectivity, they have become socially organized.

To this extent, therefore, I would underwrite the Mertonian position (Merton 1973) that crucial to the understanding of the success of modern science—of its capacity to advance knowledge—is an understanding of the distinctive institutions through which science as a social activity is conducted and of the guiding norms that these institutions express and sustain.[17] However, as a rational action theorist rather than a functionalist, I cannot here avoid a further question. Why should it be that sociologists concerned with social mobility have been more inclined than others to work within the kind of context in which a cumulative growth of knowledge is favored—why have they tended more often than others to find that the costs of conforming with the associated normative constraints have been outweighed by the benefits? This is a question for another occasion; but it is one to which an answer, if it could be provided, would, I believe, throw much light on the present state of sociology.

Notes

1. The "authority" chiefly invoked in support would appear to be Giddens and, specifically, his thesis (1984, 1987) of the "double hermeneutic." This thesis holds not only that all social science concepts must be "parasitic" on lay concepts but further that, in so far as they then serve to refine or correct the latter, they are

absorbed back into social life and its everyday interpretation, thus changing the sociologist's object of study. However, this thesis is itself open to serious challenge, not least on empirical grounds (see further below); and Giddens himself seems quite ambivalent on the implications of the thesis, if accepted, for the relationship between the natural and the social sciences. I would further note that although the authors referred to in the text emphasize their ontological concerns, they do also favor a particular epistemological stance: that is, anti-foundationalist pragmatism, especially as expressed by Rorty (1980), which entails, among other things, a rejection of the "correspondence theory" of truth. It may be useful background to this chapter if I say that I would broadly adhere to the position set out by Searle (1995) that while there is a category of social or institutional facts that differ from "brute" facts in being dependent on human agreement or acceptance, and that can therefore be understood as *ontologically subjective*, this does not prevent such "socially constructed" reality from being treated as *epistemologically objective*. Thus, a version of the correspondence theory of truth is still viable "as a methodological tool for the investigation of social facts" (Searle 1995: 200). This would seem to me to be close to the position taken up by Max Weber in the face of earlier efforts at the radical separation of *Geisteswissenschaften* and *Naturwissenschaften*.

2. Voas (2003) has recently pointed out the dispiritingly limited ambition entailed in this view in critical commentary on Jenkins (2002). It implies in effect that sociology can aspire to be little more than an intellectualized version of what, in British secondary schools in the 1950s, used to be called "civics"—classes in which, in my experience, were chiefly an occasion for surreptitious reading of the latest sports magazine or trying to arrange dates.

3. Both in including women and recording life history data, the Glass study was ahead of its time—but not in a highly productive way. On the one hand, the majority of women covered had very limited or discontinuous employment histories and no acceptable way was apparently found of handling this problem conceptually or analytically. On the other hand, data management methods available at the time could not adequately cope with the volume and complexity of life histories. Not surprisingly, little use was made of either of these features of the dataset.

4. This is, of course, what would be expected under the correspondence theory of truth. There may be many different ways of viewing the mountain—more or less revealing for the particular purposes one has in mind—but it is still the same mountain, and different perspectives on it should in principle be reconcilable.

5. Some forceful criticism has in fact been made of this "two-point" approach to the analysis of mobility (see esp. Sørensen 1986). However, this has so far had less impact than might have been anticipated for, I think, two reasons. First, because some of the more serious problems that could in principle arise with two-point analyses appear in practice to be often not all that damaging (cf. Tåhlin 1991); and second, because, although some headway has been made—as, for example, via event history analysis—technical difficulties still remain with treatment

of mobility over multiple points, leading some researchers to recommended a return, at least temporarily, to more descriptive methods, such as those of "optimal matching" (Halpin and Chan 1998; Abbott and Tsay 2000). However, it might be predicted that work-life mobility will be a major growth area over the next decade or so.

6. One outstanding problem is, however, that of developing a method analogous to path analysis—that is, that allows for the separation of direct and indirect effects—within the context of logistic regression. So far, the most notable contribution in this regard is Winship and Mare (1983).

7. It has also been a frequent finding that little variation in the pattern of relative rates occurs among different subpopulations *within* national societies. For example, few differences show up as between urban and rural areas or among geographical regions, and gender differences are slight—women showing, if anything, a weaker association between origins and destinations than men. Significant intrasocietal variation seems most common among ethno-religious communities but even then is typically quite small.

8. As regards the effects of political regimes, particular interest has attached to the efforts of (some) east-European Communist states in the decades after the World War II to increase social fluidity and create a new workers and peasants intelligentsia. Despite the degree of control that these regimes exerted over both educational and employment systems, the degree of their success was still quite limited (see esp. Szelényi 1998).

9. Of particular interest here is the application of the concept of class in the study of societies such as Japan in which, according to "area specialists," it is quite alien. However, if this is so and if sociological analysis necessarily depends on lay concepts, then nonsense results might be to be produced where mobility research is based on this concept. But in fact the results of such research show the Japanese endogenous mobility regime both to be highly stable and also to follow essentially the Western pattern (see Erikson and Goldthorpe 1992: ch. 10; Ishida 1995). More generally in this regard it may be noted that a particularly forceful counterexample to arguments such as those of Giddens is the effective use made of the concepts and theories of present-day economics in the study of the economic history of medieval and ancient societies. As Voas (2003) pertinently asks, would one really want to study the economy of ancient Babylon only in terms that would have been familiar to Nebuchadnezzar? And one might further ask how in historical sociology the "double hermeneutic" is in any case supposed to operate.

10. An argument in favor of such a tendency was advanced by Ganzeboom et al. (1989; and cf. also Treiman and Ganzeboom 2000) but has been subject to strong criticism, including by Jones (1992), Erikson and Goldthorpe (1992), and Wong (1994).

11. In other words, the "feedback loop" problem in functional explanation, as identified by Stinchcombe (1968) and Elster (1979), was fully apparent: that is,

the problem of showing how, if X has an effect Y that is beneficial for the functioning of the system Z, Y in turn maintains X by some feedback loop passing through Z.

12. The role played by Boudon in arguing for new micro-theoretical effort in social mobility research has been of general importance, although his arguments were initially directed not so much against functionalist explanations as against a form of "variable sociology" that supposed that causal explanations could be simply cranked out of statistical analysis without need for theory of any kind. See the celebrated debate between Boudon (1976) and Hauser (1976). Such an overestimation of what can be achieved by statistical analysis—most common, it seems, among American sociologists—remains perhaps the main obstacle in the way of further theoretical advance in mobility research.

13. Cole seems not to consider this possibility. He takes general theory to be chiefly exemplified by the work of such authors as Parsons, Giddens, and Alexander, in which, as he rightly argues, the degree of generality sought at the level of concepts undermines explanatory power—and, I would add, in which conceptualization appears to become an end in itself, superseding that of explanation.

14. Thus, Flyvbjerg (2001) recurrently takes the failure of sociology to develop theories that allow prediction as being the leading indicator of its qualitative difference from the natural sciences—even while at one point (p. 39) acknowledging that in some natural sciences prediction "is relatively rare." Essentially the same line of argument is found in Jenkins (2002). What appears to be neglected here is that prediction in the natural sciences, insofar as it occurs, typically takes place within closed systems—as may be set up in laboratories—and not in the kind of open system with which sociologists have usually to deal. And if, in regard to the latter context, one thinks of forecasting rather than prediction, it is not clear that sociology is always at a disadvantage as compared with the natural sciences. I would be ready to bet against any meteorologist that I would do better as of now (April) at forecasting traffic conditions in central Oxford next Christmas Day than he or she would at forecasting weather conditions.

15. Such a mode of explanation is now in fact being increasingly proposed, mainly by European sociologists, as one of general relevance and value for sociology. See for example Blossfeld and Prein (1998), Hedström and Swedberg (1998), Goldthorpe (2000), and Boudon (2002, 2003). For the importance of sociologists looking to biology rather than physics for their models of science, see Lieberson and Lynn (2002).

16. It is my—highly unfashionable—skepticism regarding the Kuhnian approach to the history and philosophy of science (and my absolute conviction regarding its deleterious effects on sociology) that lead me to speak of a "tradition" of social mobility research, which can evolve without serious problems of "incommensurability," rather than a "paradigm," subject to total overthrow.

17. Indeed, the specific norms identified by Merton as forming the institutionalized ethos of science could, I believe, all be shown to operate within the RC28

collectivity—with, of course, a normal amount of individual deviance: that is, universalism—the rejection of the idea that truth claims in any way depend on the personal or social attributes of those making them; "communism"—in the sense that all research results, as a product of collaborative activity, should be available in the public domain; "disinterestedness"—in the sense of a rejection of fraud, deceit, grandstanding, etc. for personal advantage; organized skepticism—as a methodological mandate; and "humility"—in the sense of a recognition of working within, and being indebted to, a tradition rather than seeking to create one's own system de novo.

References

Abbott, A. and Tsay, A. 2000. Sequence Analysis and Optimal Matching Methods in Sociology (with discussion). *Sociological Methods and Research* 29: 3–33.

Becker, R. 2003. Educational Expansion and Persistent Inequalities of Education in Germany. *European Sociological Review* 19:1–24.

Bell, D. 1973. *The Coming of Post-Industrial Society* New York: Basic Books.

Bell D. 1980. Liberalism in the Post-Industrial Society. In *Sociological Journeys*. London: Heinemann.

Blau, P. M. and Duncan, O. D. 1967. *The American Occupational Structure*. New York: Wiley.

Blossfeld, H.-P. and Shavit, Y. (eds.). 1993. *Persistent Inequality: Changing Educational Attainment in Thirteen Countries*. Boulder, Colo.: Westview.

Blossfeld, H.-P. and Prein, G. (eds.). 1998. *Rational Choice Theory and Large-Scale Data Analysis*. Boulder, Colo.: Westview.

Boudon, R. 1974. *Education, Opportunity and Social Inequality*. New York: Wiley.

Boudon, R. 1976. Comment on Hauser's Review of Education, Opportunity and Social Inequality. *American Journal of Sociology* 81:1175–1187.

Boudon, R. 1998. Social Mechanisms Without Black Boxes. In P. Hedström and R. Swedberg (eds.) *Social Mechanisms*. Cambridge: Cambridge University Press.

Boudon, R. 2002. Sociology that Really Matters. *European Sociological Review* 18:371–378.

Boudon, R. 2003. Beyond Rational Choice Theory. *Annual Review of Sociology* 29:1–21.

Brauns, H. and Steinmann, S. 1999. Educational Reform in France, West Germany and the United Kingdom: Updating the CASMIN Educational Classification. *ZUMA-Nachrichtung* 44:7–44.

Breen, R. 1994. Individual Level Models for Mobility Tables and other Cross-Classifications. *Sociological Methods and Research* 23:147–173.

Breen, R. 2001. A Rational Choice Model of Educational Inequality, Istituto Juan March, Madrid, Working Paper 2001/166.

Breen R. (ed.). 2004. *Social Mobility in Europe*. Oxford: Oxford University Press.

Breen, R. and Goldthorpe, J. H. 1997. Explaining Educational Differentials: Towards a Formal Rational Choice Theory. *Rationality and Society* 9:275–305.

Breen, R. and Goldthorpe, J. H. 1999. Class Inequality and Meritocracy: A Critique of Saunders and an Alternative Analysis. *British Journal of Sociology* 50:1–27.

Breen, R. and Goldthorpe, J. H. 2001. Class, Mobility and Merit: The Experience of Two British Birth Cohorts. *European Sociological Review* 17:81–101.

Breen, R. and Jonsson, J. O. 1997. How Reliable Are Studies of Social Mobility? *Research in Social Stratification and Mobility* 15:91–112.

Breen, R. and Jonsson, J. O. 2003. Period and Cohort Change in Social Fluidity: Sweden 1976–1999. Working Paper, Nuffield College, Oxford.

Breen, R. and Yaish, M. 2006. Testing the Breen-Goldthorpe Model of Educational Decision Making. In S. L. Morgan, Grusky, D. B., and Fields, G. S. (eds.), *Mobility and Inequality: Frontiers of Research from Sociology and Economics*. Stanford: Stanford University Press.

Breen, R. and Luijkx, R. Forthcoming. Conclusions. In Breen R. (ed.), *Social Mobility in Europe*. Oxford: Oxford University Press.

Bryant, C. G. A. 1995. *Practical Sociology*. Cambridge: Polity.

Carlsson, G. 1958. *Social Mobility and Class Structure*. Lund: Gleerup.

Cole, S. 1992. *Making Science: Between Nature and Society*. Cambridge, Mass.: Harvard University Press.

Cole, S. 1994. Why Sociology Doesn't Make Progress Like the Natural Sciences. *Sociological Forum* 9:133–154.

Coleman, J. S. 1990. *Foundations of Social Theory*. Cambridge, Mass.: Belknap.

Cox, D. R. 1992. Causality: Some Statistical Aspects. *Journal of the Royal Statistical Society*, Series A 155:291–301.

Crump, T. 2002. *A Brief History of Science as Seen Through the Development of Scientific Instruments*. London: Robinson.

Davies, R., Heinesen, H., and Holm, A. 2002. The Relative Risk Aversion Hypothesis. *Journal of Population Economics* 15:683–713.

Duncan, O. D. and Hodge, R. 1963. Education and Occupational Mobility: A Regression Analysis. *American Journal of Sociology* 68:629–649.

Elster, J. 1979. *Ulysses and the Sirens*. Cambridge: Cambridge University Press.

Erikson, R. 1990. Politics and Class Mobility—Does Politics Influence Rates of Social Mobility? In I. Persson (ed.), *Generating Inequality in the Welfare State*. Oslo: Norwegian University Press.

Erikson, R. and Goldthorpe, J. H. 1992a. *The Constant Flux: A Study of Class Mobility in Industrial Societies*. Oxford: Clarendon.

Featherman, D. L., Jones, F. L., and Hauser, R. M. 1975. Assumptions of Social Mobility Research in the US: The Case of Occupational Status. *Social Science Research* 4:329–360.

Flyvbjerg, B. 2001. *Making Social Science Matter* Cambridge: Cambridge University Press.

Ganzeboom, H. G. B., Luijkx, R., and Treiman, D. J. 1989. Intergenerational Class Mobility in Comparative Perspective. *Research in Social Stratification and Mobility* 8:3–55.

Ganzeboom, H. G. B., Treiman, D. J., and Ultee, W. C. 1991. Comparative Intergenerational Stratification Research: Three Generations and Beyond. *Annual Review of Sociology* 17:277–302.

Ganzeboom, H. B. G. and Treiman, D. J. 1996. Internationally Comparable Measures of Occupational Status for the 1988 International Standard Classification of Occupations. *Social Science Research* 25:201–239.

Giddens, A. 1984. *The Constitution of Society*. Cambridge: Polity.

Giddens, A. 1987. *Social Theory and Modern Sociology*. Cambridge: Polity.

Glass, D. V. (ed.). 1954. *Social Mobility in Britain*. London: Routledge.

Goldthorpe, J. H. (with Llewellyn, C. and Payne, C.). 1980/1987. *Social Mobility and Class Structure in Modern Britain*. Oxford: Clarendon.

Goldthorpe, J. H. 2000. *On Sociology: Numbers, Narratives and the Integration of Research and Theory*. Oxford: Oxford University Press.

Grusky, D. and Hauser, R. M. 1984. Comparative Social Mobility Revisited: Models of Convergence and Divergence in 16 Countries. *American Sociological Review* 49:19–38.

Guzzo, S. 2002. Getting in Through the Back Door: Equal Educational Qualifications, Unequal Occupational Returns. ISA Research Committee on Social Stratification and Mobility, Oxford.

Halpin, B. and Chan, T-W. 1998. Class Careers as Sequences: An Optimal Matching Analysis of Work-Life Histories. *European Sociological Review* 14:111–130.

Hauser, R. M. 1976. On Boudon's Model of Social Mobility. *American Journal of Sociology* 81:911–928.

Hauser, R. M. 1978. A Structural Model of the Mobility Table. *Social Forces* 56:919–953.

Hauser, R. M., Dickinson, P. J., Travis, H. P., and Koffel, J. M. 1975. Temporal Change in Occupational Mobility: Evidence for Men in the United States. *American Sociological Review* 40:279–297.

Hedström, P. and Swedberg, R. (eds.). 1998. *Social Mechanisms*. Cambridge: Cambridge University Press.

Hendrickx, J. and Ganzeboom, H. G. B. 1998. Occupational Status Attainment in the Netherlands, 1920–1990: A Multinomial Logistic Analysis. *European Sociological Review* 14:387–403.

Hillmert, S. and Jacob, M. 2003. Social Inequality in Higher Education: Is Vocational Training a Pathway Leading to or away from University? *European Sociological Review* 19:319–34.

Hope, K., Schwartz, J., and Graham, S. 1986. Uncovering the Pattern of Social

Stratification: A Two-Year Test-Retest Inquiry. *British Journal of Sociology* 37:397–430.

Hout, M. 1988. More Universalism, Less Structural Mobility: The American Occupational Structure in the 1980s. *American Journal of Sociology* 93:1358–1400.

Hout, M. and DiPrete, T. A. 2000. What We have Learned: RC28's Contribution to Knowledge About Social Stratification. Department of Sociology, University of California, Berkeley.

Ishida, H. 1995. Intergenerational Class Mobility and Reproduction. In Ishida (ed.), *Social Stratification and Mobility: Basic Analysis and Cross-National Comparison*. Tokyo: SSM Research Series.

Ishida, H., Müller, W., and Ridge J. M. 1995. Class Origin, Class Destination, and Education: A Cross-National Study of Ten Industrial Nations. *American Journal of Sociology* 60:145–93.

Jackson, M., Goldthorpe, J. H., and Mills, C. 2005. Education, Employers and Class Mobility. *Research in Social Stratification and Mobility* 24:1–35.

Jenkins, R. 2002. *Foundations of Sociology*. Basingstoke: Palgrave Macmillan.

Jones, F. L. 1992. Common Social Fluidity: A Comment on Recent Criticisms. *European Sociological Review* 8:255–259.

Jonsson, J. O. and Erikson, R. 2000. Understanding Educational Inequality: The Swedish Experience. *L'année sociologique* 50:345–382.

Jonsson, J. O. 2004. Equality at Halt? Social Mobility in Sweden, 1976–99. In R. Breen (ed.), *National Patterns of Social Mobility: Convergence or Divergence?* Oxford: Oxford University Press.

Kerr, C., Dunlop, J. T., Harbison, F. H., and Myers, C. A. 1960/1973. *Industrialism and Industrial Man*. 2nd Ed. Cambridge: Harvard University Press.

König, W., Lüttinger, P., and Müller, W. 1988. A Comparative Analysis of the Development and Structure of Educational Systems: Methodological Foundations and the Construction of a Comparative Educational Scale. CASMIN Working Paper 12, University of Mannheim.

Kurz, K. and Müller, W. 1987. Class Mobility in the Industrial World. *Annual Review of Sociology* 13:417–442.

Lieberson, S. and Lynn, F. B. 2002. Barking up the Wrong Branch: Scientific Alternatives to the Current Model of Sociological Science. *Annual Review of Sociology* 28:1–19.

Lipset, S. M. and Zetterberg, H. L. 1956. A Theory of Social Mobility. *Transactions of the Third World Congress of Sociology*, vol. III. London: International Sociological Association.

Logan, J. A. 1983. A Multivariate Model for Mobility Tables. *American Journal of Sociology* 89:324–349.

Marshall, G., Swift, A., and Roberts, S. 1997. *Against the Odds: Social Class and Social Justice in Industrial Societies*. Oxford: Clarendon.

Medawar, P. 1958. *Pluto's Republic*. Oxford: Oxford University Press.

Merton, R. K. 1973. *The Sociology of Science*. Chicago: Chicago University Press.

Miller, R. 1998. The Limited Concerns of Social Mobility Research. *Current Sociology* 46:145–163.

Parsons, T. 1960. *Structure and Process in Modern Societies*. Glencoe, Ill.: Free Press.

Popper, K. R. 1976. *Unended Quest*. London: Fontana.

Popper, K. R. 1994. *The Myth of the Framework*. London: Routledge.

Rijken, S. 1999. *Educational Expansion and Status Attainment*. Utrecht: ICS.

Rorty, R. 1980. *Philosophy and the Mirror of Nature*. Oxford: Blackwell.

Rule, J. B. 1997. *Theory and Progress in Social Science*. Cambridge: Cambridge University Press.

Schizzerotto, A. 1997. Perche. In Italia ci sono pochi diplomati e pochi laureate? Vincoli strutturali e decisioni razionali degli attori come cause delle contenuta espansione della scolarite' superiore, *Polis* 11:345–365.

Searle, J. R. 1995. *The Construction of Social Reality*. London: Allen Lane.

Sørensen, A. B. 1986. Theory and Methodology in Social Stratification. In U. Himmelstrand (ed.), *Sociology from Crisis to Science?* London: Sage.

Sorokin, P. A. 1927/1959. *Social Mobility*. Glencoe, Ill.: Free Press.

Stinchcombe, A. L. 1968. *Constructing Social Theories*. New York: Harcourt Brace.

Steuer, M. 2002. *The Scientific Study of Society*. Boston: Kluwer.

Svalastoga, K. 1959. *Prestige, Class and Mobility*. Copenhagen: Gyldendal.

Szelényi, S. 1998. *Equality by Design: The Grand Experiment in Destratification in Socialist Hungary*. Stanford: Stanford University Press.

Tåhlin, M. 1991. Class Mobility in a Swedish City. In E. J. Hansen, S. Ringen, H. Uusitalo, and R. Erikson (eds.), *Scandinavian Trends in Welfare and Living Conditions*. Armonk, NY: Sharpe.

Treiman, D. J. 1970. Industrialization and Social Stratification. In E. O. Laumann (ed.), *Social Stratification: Research and Theory for the 1970s*. Indianapolis: Bobbs-Merrill.

Treiman, D. J. 1977. *Occupational Prestige in Comparative Perspective*. New York: Academic Press.

Treiman, D. J. and Ganzeboom, H. G. B. 2000. The Fourth Generation of Comparative Stratification Research. In S. R. Quah and A. Sales (eds.), *The International Handbook of Sociology*. London: Sage.

Vallet, L.-A. 2004. Change in Intergenerational Class Mobility in France from the 1970s to the 1990s and Its Explanation. In R. Breen (ed.), *Social Mobility in Europe*. Oxford: Oxford University Press.

Voas, D. 2003. The So-So Construction of Sociology. *British Journal of Sociology* 54:129–137.

Winship, C. and Mare, R. D. 1983. Structural Equations and Path Analysis for Discrete Data. *American Journal of Sociology* 89:54–110.

Wolpert, L. 1992. *The Unnatural Nature of Science*. London: Faber.

Wong R. S-K. 1990. Understanding Cross-National Variation in Occupational Mobility. *American Sociological Review* 55:560–573.

Wong, R. S-K. 1994. Postwar Mobility Trends in Advanced Industrial Societies. *Research in Social Stratification and Mobility* 13:121–144.

CHAPTER FOUR

Social Indicators, Policy, and Measuring Progress

A. B. Atkinson

This chapter is about the relation between social science and policy,[1] connecting specifically with some of the important themes of the analysis of inequality: the measurement of welfare, comparative social research, and change over time. These factors come together in the development of international social indicators, which have risen to prominence in recent years. The chapter takes as its point of departure two important policy areas where social indicators have been used in a serious way and where the methods adopted are likely to influence the future actions of national governments and international bodies. The *first* of these is the adoption of social indicators by the European Union (EU) as part of the development of Social Europe. Following the 2000 Lisbon European Council, the EU has agreed on a set of commonly defined social indicators for use in comparing the performance of member states and evaluating progress. The European Commission is charged with producing an annual scoreboard. The *second* is the adoption by the United Nations of the Millennium Development Goals (MDGs). At the Millennium Summit in September 2000, the 189 states of the United Nations affirmed their commitment to sustained development and the eradication of world poverty. These goals are expressed in terms of a concrete set of indicators, with agreed targets, notably the halving, between 1990 and 2015, of the proportion of people who live on less than $1 a day.

The first section of the chapter outlines the history and nature of the social indicators used in the two cases, and their relation to the policy process. An important function has been that of raising consciousness of the extent of social problems, and persuading political leaders to give them greater priority. In this, the EU social indicators and the MDGs have been, in my view, a "qualified success" (second section). At the same time, the link between indicators and the design of policy is, in both cases, problematic (third section). Indeed, there is a certain irony in the adoption in 2000 by the EU, and by the world as a whole, of an approach to governance reminiscent of the former Communist bloc. Moreover, in both cases, the stimulus to policy action has come from an assessment of the *current state* of the world. It is the level of world poverty, and the extent of social exclusion in Europe, that has led to political action. It is, however, *changes over time* that are important in monitoring progress. The exercise of measuring change is a different one from measuring levels and may require an alternative approach (fourth section). The purpose of this evaluation of social indicators is to raise a number of critical questions, but I am seeking to be a sympathetic critic, because I believe that social indicators have an important role to play, both in Europe and at a world level. Moreover, as indicated in the concluding section, I believe that social science can contribute to the resolution of the problems raised. Social indicators have a substantial political ingredient, but they are not purely politics.

SOCIAL INDICATORS AND WORLD POVERTY MEASURES

The two policy applications of social indicators considered in this chapter are, of course, quite different. The poverty line used in the European Union is more like $15–$20 a day than $1 a day. The MDGs have a global reach, whereas European social policy is a regional preoccupation. The UN has set specific goals, whereas the EU member states have resisted setting social targets at the EU level. Nevertheless, I believe setting the two processes alongside each other can be instructive.[2]

Social Indicators and the European Union

In its evaluation of the first European Action Programme on Poverty, the European Commission estimated that in 1975 some 37 million people in the Community (then 12 countries) were living in poverty. This estimate was based on a poverty line drawn at 50 percent of mean income of the member state, which was the concrete implementation of the definition adopted by the Council of Ministers of the poor as "individuals or families whose resources are so small as to exclude them from the minimal acceptable way of life of the Member State in which they live" (Council Decision, July 22,

1975, see European Commission 1985), a definition that has been widely quoted and widely influential. This estimate made a quarter century ago may be seen as the origin of the common EU indicators for social inclusion agreed on in December 2001. In between, there have of course been a number of stages. The Final Report on the Second Programme, taking expenditure rather than income as the indicator of resources, reached the alternative estimate for 1985 of 50 million people, based on the study carried out by Hagenaars, de Vos, and Zaidi (1994). These statistics referred to monetary poverty, but there was at the same time an increasing appreciation of the multidimensional nature of deprivation. Concern in France with social exclusion and precariousness led to the Commission's emphasizing the significance of new forms of poverty. Sweden, long before joining the European Union, had moved beyond purely monetary indicators to a broader concept of social welfare: "In 1954 an expert group within the United Nations suggested that we should not rely on monetary measures alone: the measurement of well-being should be based on several different components. . . . Partly influenced by the UN expert group, Johansson made level of living, seen as a set of components, the basic concept in the first Swedish Level of Living Survey conducted in 1968" (Erikson 1993, p. 67).

These two strands—measures of monetary poverty and stress on multidimensionality—have been taken forward in recent developments. Following Lisbon, it was agreed to advance social policy on the basis of an *open method of coordination*, an approach recognizing that, under the principle of subsidiarity, social policy remains the responsibility of member states. The process of open coordination involves fixing guidelines for the Union, establishing quantitative and qualitative indicators to be applied in each member state, and periodic monitoring. The European Commission is invited to identify good practice and to promote its common acceptance. The same process has been in operation in the field of employment, and just as in the case of employment, it was decided that each member state should implement a *national action plan (NAP)*. The first national action plans on social inclusion were submitted by the fifteen member states in June 2001; they were reviewed in the *Joint Report on Social Inclusion* (European Commission, 2002). Member states submitted the second set of national action plans/inclusion in the summer of 2003.

Social indicators are playing an important role in this process. At the Nice European Council, the European Commission was requested to monitor the implementation of the social agenda and to prepare an annual score-board of progress. In order to achieve these goals, the EU Social Protection Committee established a subgroup on social indicators. The results of the work of the group (Social Protection Committee, 2001) were accepted by the Employment and Social Affairs Council in December 2001, and now form the basis for European Union policy making. The primary indicators (see Table 4.1) encompass financial poverty, income inequality, regional var-iation in employment rates, long-term unemployment, joblessness, low edu-cational qualifications, life expectancy, and poor health. In a number of cases, breakdowns show, for example, poverty among men and women or categories by age.

Agreement on a common set of indicators was seen by some as a step toward agreement on targets. Indeed, the Barcelona European Council in spring 2002 invited member states "to set targets, in their national action plans, for significantly reducing the number of people at risk of poverty and social exclusion by 2010" (Social Protection Committee, 2003, Appendix I). The Common Outline for the 2003/2005 NAPs/inclusion explains that such targets are important for several reasons. National targets are "a significant political statement of purpose" and provide "a goal against which to mea-sure progress" (Social Protection Committee, 2003, Appendix I). Yet mem-ber states, with some notable exceptions such as Ireland (see Nolan 1999) and the UK, have been reluctant nationally to set time-specific targets for the reduction in the number of people at risk of poverty or social exclusion. EU leaders have not set targets for the EU as a whole.

World Poverty and the Millennium Development Goals

Neither body would perhaps appreciate the comparison, but the role of the commission in developing poverty statistics for the EU has a parallel in the work of the World Bank, in conjunction with other international organiza-tions such as the United Nations Development Programme (UNDP), in de-veloping statistics on world poverty. In 1990 the World Bank devoted its an-nual World Development Report to the problem of poverty. When discussing poverty within countries, it made use of country-specific poverty lines, but "a universal poverty line is needed to permit cross-country comparison and aggregation" (World Bank 1990, p. 27). Comparing across countries re-quired adjustment for differences in purchasing power not reflected in exchange rates. Recognizing that such a line is "somewhat arbitrary," the

TABLE 4.1
Primary Indicators for Social Inclusion
Adopted by the European Union 2001

	Indicator	Definition
1.	At-Risk-of-Poverty Rate After Social Transfers	Share of Persons Living in Households with an Income Below 60% National Median Income (Breakdowns by Age and Gender, Most Frequent Activity Status, Household Type, Tenure Status + Illustrative Values of the At-Risk-of-Poverty Threshold)
2.	Inequality of Income Distribution	Ratio of Total Income Received by the Top 20% of the Country's Population with the Highest Income (Top Quintile) to That Received by the 20% of the Country's Population with the Lowest Income (Bottom Quintile)
3.	Persistent Risk-of-Poverty Rate (60% Median)	Share of Persons Living in Households with an Income Below the 60% Risk-of-Poverty Threshold in Current Year and in at Least Two of the Preceding Years (Incl. Gender Breakdown)
4.	Relative Median At-Risk-of-Poverty Gap	Difference Between the Median Income of Persons Below the Low Income Threshold and the At-Risk-of-Poverty Threshold, Expressed as a Percentage of this Threshold (Incl. Gender Breakdown)
5.	Regional Cohesion	Coefficient of Variation of Employment Rates at NUTS 2 Level
6.	Long-Term Unemployment Rate	Total Long-Term Unemployed Population ($\geq$12 Months; ILO Definition) as Proportion of Total Active Population (Incl. Gender Breakdown)
7.	Persons Living in Jobless Households	Persons Age 0–65 (0–60) Living in Households Where None Is Working out of the Persons Living in Eligible Households
8.	Early School Leavers Not in Education or Training	Share of Total Population of 18–24-Year Olds Having Achieved ISCED Level 2 or Less and Not Attending Education or Training (Incl. Gender Breakdown)
9.	Life Expectancy at Birth	Number of Years a Person May Be Expected to Live, Starting at Age 0, for Males and Females
10.	Self-Defined Health Status by Income Level	Ratio of the Proportions in the Bottom and Top Income Quintile Groups (by Equivalised Income) of the Population Age 16 and Over Who Classify Themselves as in a Bad or Very Bad State of Health (Incl. Gender Breakdown)

NOTE: "Income" is defined as the household's total disposable income divided by its "equivalent size," to take account of the size and composition of the household, and is attributed to each household member including children.

World Bank employed two lines: $275 and $370 per person per year in constant 1985 purchasing power prices. The range "was chosen to span the poverty lines estimated in recent studies for a number of countries with low average incomes. [The lower limit] coincides with a poverty line commonly used for India" (World Bank 1990: 27).

The 2000 World Development Report returned to the problem of poverty, using $1 a day and $2 a day poverty lines, the former an approximation to the $1.08 a day calculated by Chen and Ravallion (2001), and the latter obtained "by doubling the amount of the lower poverty line" (World Bank, 2001, Box 1.2). The 2000 report stressed the multidimensional nature of poverty. Its overview described seven international development goals, with social indicators for each. Income poverty is one of these indicators, but so too are primary school enrollment rates, under-5 mortality rates, and the proportion of countries with strategies for sustainable development. The international development goals became the Millennium Development Goals, set out in Table 4.2.

In the case of the MDG, in contrast to the EU case, social indicators are linked explicitly to targets. This is not the only respect in which the processes are different. They have, however, in common that the indicators have been agreed on, with a common definition, by heads of state and government. They share the fact that they relate to a multigovernment policy process, and rest on an acceptance by nation-states that they have a responsibility for those living in other countries. This recognition is explicit in the development context, where the MDGs can be expected to influence the development assistance policies of rich countries. In the EU, disparities between member states are much less marked (although becoming greater with enlargement), but there is an implicit acceptance of a degree of shared responsibility.

CONSCIOUSNESS RAISING: A QUALIFIED SUCCESS

The degree of political acceptance of the EU and MDG indicators is remarkable, given the fragile nature of multilateral collaboration in today's world. This success has been achieved in large part because the indicators provided a powerful rallying point. In the case of the European Union, Jacques Delors, as Commission president, employed the statistics for the number living in poverty to considerable effect, to motivate the development

TABLE 4.2
Summary of Millennium Development Goals

Goal	
Goal 1: Eradicate Extreme Poverty and Hunger	Halve, Between 1990 and 2015, the Proportion of People Whose Income Is Less Than $1 a Day. Halve, Between 1990 and 2015, the Proportion of People Who Suffer from Hunger.
Goal 2: Achieve Universal Primary Education	Ensure that by 2015 All Children Will Be Able to Complete a Full Course of Primary Schooling.
Goal 3: Promote Gender Equality and Empower Women	Eliminate Gender Disparity in All Levels of Education by 2015.
Goal 4: Reduce Child Mortality	Reduce by Two-Thirds, Between 1990 and 2015, the Under-5 Mortality Rate.
Goal 5: Improve Maternal Health	Reduce by Three-Quarters, Between 1990 and 2015, the Maternal Mortality Ratio.
Goal 6: Combat HIV/AIDS, Malaria, and Other Diseases	Have Halted by 2015 and Begun to Reverse the Spread of HIV/AIDS. Have Halted by 2015 and Begun to Reverse the Spread of Malaria and Other Major Diseases.
Goal 7: Ensure Environmental Sustainability	Integrate Principles of Sustainable Development into Country Policies and Reverse the Loss of Environmental Resources. Halve, by 2015, the Proportion of People Without Sustainable Access to Safe Drinking Water. Have Achieved, by 2020, a Significant Improvement in the Lives of at Least 100 Million Slum Dwellers.
Goal 8: Develop a Global Partnership for Development	Develop the World Trading and Financial System. Address the Special Needs of the Least Developed and Landlocked and Small Island Countries. Deal Comprehensively with the Debt Problems of Developing Countries.

of the social agenda. Politicians concerned about social issues have drawn a parallel with the use of indicators and the setting of targets in the macro-economic field as part of the Maastricht process. The Lisbon process has changed both attitudes and institutions (such as the establishment of the Social Protection Committee). The open method of coordination has many critics, but it is interesting that those who regard the process as ineffective are counterbalanced by those who feel that it has been too effective, taking power away from the European Parliament. Success in placing poverty and social exclusion on the agenda has, of course, required the building of coalitions. Here, the twin strategy of quoting "hard" numbers on income poverty, while stressing the multidimensionality of deprivation, has appealed to differing national approaches.

Equally, in the case of global poverty, there can be little doubt that the use of social indicators has helped galvanize action by policy makers. The number of people living on less than $1 a day has been used by the World Bank president, and other campaigners, to raise public awareness. The citizens of rich countries, aware in many cases that official development assistance had been falling in their countries as a percentage of gross domestic product (GDP), used the indicators to stimulate increased private action, and to bring pressure on their governments. For the international institutions, the MDGs have provided a policy framework. As described by the World Bank: "the goals focus the efforts of the world community on achieving significant, measurable improvements in people's lives. They establish yardsticks for measuring results not just for developing countries but for the rich countries that help to fund development programs and for the multilateral institutions that help countries implement them" (World Bank website, October 14, 2003).

Inputs and Outputs

Social indicators have proved therefore to be powerful instruments in public debate; at the same time, they need to be applied with care. Their use in the policy process has revealed some of their limitations. Here I set out three reasons why I believe the indicators have been only a qualified success: the elision of inputs and outputs, the rush to aggregate indicators, and the ambivalence regarding nationality.

Table 4.2 shows that the majority of MDG indicators relate to outcomes: for example, halving the proportion of people without sustainable access to safe drinking water. But other indicators relate to policy inputs: for example, integrating principles of sustainable development into country policies. Reference is often made to increasing official development assistance, but this is an input not an output. In the EU case, the indicators listed in Table 4.1 are concerned with outputs, but the national action plans of member states make use of both performance (output) indicators and policy effort (input) indicators. For the 2003 NAPs/inclusion, the common outline states "performance or outcome indicators are strongly preferred [but] policy effort indicators could be used when performance or outcome indicators are not measurable" (Social Protection Committee, 2003: 6). However, it is important to keep them separate, not least because input indicators are more readily available than those on outputs. As was noted in the U.S. *Toward a Social Report* over 30 years ago, the annual statistics on education contained over a hundred pages, "yet has virtually no information on how much children have learned" (U.S. Department of Health, Education, and Welfare 1969: 66). The separation of inputs and outputs is particularly relevant to the European Union, where the principle of subsidiarity in the social field means that policy effort as such is not the subject of evaluation. Member states can legitimately differ in their choice of means to combat poverty. To take an example, the replacement rate in a state pension scheme may be lower in one country than another because greater reliance is placed on private pension schemes. Evaluating countries on the basis of the replacement rates for the state pension would be misleading.

Stress on the distinction between input and output is one of the contributions of the social science literature, but the distinction also opens up a series of uncomfortable questions. Why, a critic may ask, is the replacement rate an input measure, but the income of the elderly an output measure? Surely income is an intermediate vehicle in achieving well-being? Income is an input, along with other components, such as public, communal, and family services. Is it not possible that some countries may make greater provision for the elderly through public services and others through larger pensions? Or, to take another example, why are we concerned about the number of people living in jobless households (Indicator 7 in Table 4.1)? Does work have an intrinsic value, over and above the wages earned? Is "work" an output because it provides social contacts and social integration? Conversely, does not the existence of social facilities have an option value? The presence of a hospital provides reassurance to the population even if the prevalence of sickness is low. These are, to my mind, open questions.

The widespread adoption of social indicators does not, therefore, mean that the tricky questions underlying the definition of social welfare have been resolved. A particular set of indicators represents one answer to those questions, an answer that has received some degree of political acceptance, but which must be open to revision. The indicators should not be regarded as set in stone, but subject to evolution, as social scientists understand more about the determinants of social well-being and as societies develop.

Aggregate Scores

Recognition of the multidimensional nature of deprivation has been an important step forward, but faced with a row of numbers, there seems to be an almost irresistible urge to aggregate them into a single index. Perhaps the best-known aggregate score is the Human Development Index (HDI) published by the UNDP since 1990, which is a composite of three basic components: longevity, knowledge, and standard of living. The rationale given in 1990 was that "too many indicators could produce a perplexing picture—perhaps distracting policymakers from the main overall trends" (UNDP 1990: 11). The addition of separate indices for gross domestic product (GDP), life expectancy, and educational attainment has certainly served to broaden the focus from looking only at GDP.

There are, however, a number of reasons why we should not rush too quickly to reduce a multidimensional phenomenon to a single number. To begin with, it is important to distinguish two different forms of aggregation. The first combines aggregate indicators, as with the HDI; the second combines different elements of deprivation at the individual level, which are then summed over individuals to form an aggregate index for the country. In a theoretical sense, this difference is simply an issue of the order of summation. Do we aggregate first across people and then across fields, or across fields for an individual and then across individuals? But there are substantive differences in the way in which investigators think about how the summation should be done. In the latter case, the issue is multiple deprivation at the level of the individual—whether the same people are suffering both income poverty and low educational attainment. An approach based on household wel-

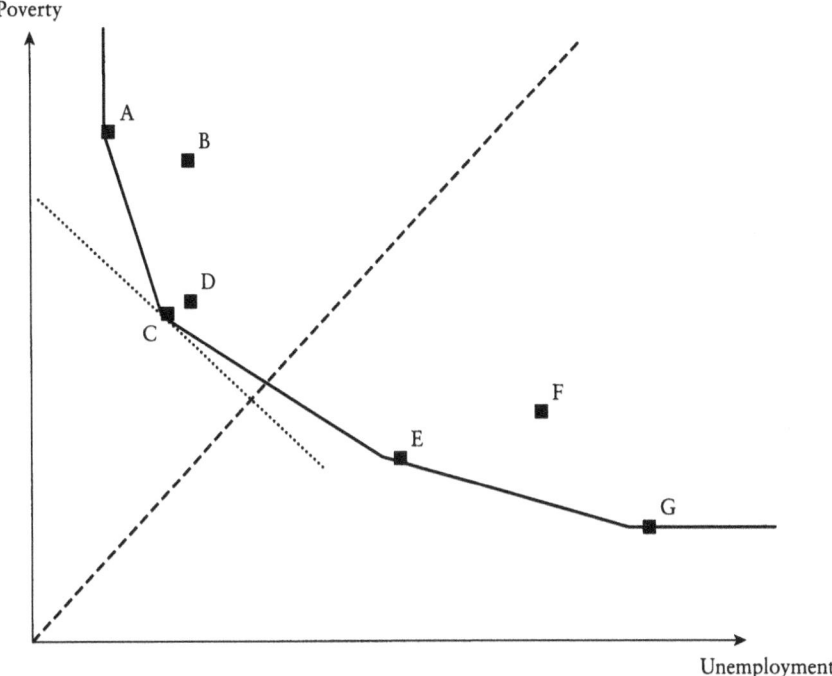

Poverty

Unemployment

Figure 4.1.   Aggregating Indicators

fare then indicates how the separate deprivations should be aggregated into a single indicator for individual households; alternatively a "counting" approach leads us to focus on those with n, $(n - 1)$, $(n - 2)$ . . . deprivations (for example, Erikson and Tåhlin 1987, Table 14.2). (See Atkinson 2003, for an analysis of the differences between these two approaches.)

Here I concentrate on the combination of aggregate indicators, which must inevitably involve social judgments. The problem is illustrated in poverty/unemployment space in Figure 4.1 for seven hypothetical countries, ranging from A ("Albion") with low unemployment but high poverty to G ("Germania") with low poverty and high unemployment. Summation, as in the HDI, adds the two scores: the social welfare contours are therefore 45° lines, and country C is ranked the highest, with D close behind. Even with a linear social welfare function, however, there is no reason why the variables should be weighted equally. If a greater weight were attached to poverty than to unemployment, so the slope of the social welfare contours is less steep, then country E could take over the lead. Moreover, why should we simply add? Alternatives to simple addition are considered, in the context of poverty indices, by Anand and Sen (1997). One limiting case is that of "Min" social welfare contours, where countries are ranked according to the dimension on which they perform least well. The space is then divided into two. Above the 45° line, poverty has priority; below the 45° line, unemployment has priority.

One problem with the choice of weights is that these may not conform with those embodied in national policy objectives. This problem has led Cherchye, Moesen, and Van Puyenbroeck (2003) to argue that the weights should vary across countries according to their own national priorities, as revealed in their performance. If a country regards poverty as more important than unemployment, then poverty should be weighted more highly when constructing the synthetic indicator for that country. Cherchye, Moesen, and Van Puyenbroeck develop this approach by drawing a parallel with data envelopment analysis in production theory. In essence, this parallel involves asking how close countries are to the "efficiency frontier," illustrated in Figure 4.1 by the frontier ACEG. All four of these countries score 100 percent, because none is dominated by another country. There is, for example, always a dimension on which Country E scores better than any other country (it beats G on unemployment and all the others on poverty). They then devise a measure of the distance by which "non-frontier" countries fall short of the frontier, obtaining the weights by solving a linear programming problem.

The efficiency frontier approach is a good example of cross-fertilization in social science, with a technique developed for one purpose being applied imaginatively to a quite different field. But I am not fully persuaded. I am not sure that policy makers would find the solution of a linear programming problem less perplexing than consideration of a number of separate indicators. It may appear to be offering a scientific resolution of what is at heart a political problem, ignoring the advice that "weighing together different welfare components should be avoided to the very last so as not to conceal dissensions in a 'scientific' model" (Erikson 1974: 279). Another possibility is to drop the linear programming element and simply rank each country on the dimension on which they perform best, measuring the distance from the best performance. But this strategy would convey the message to national governments that they did not need to make efforts to improve their performance on the other dimensions.

Ambivalence Regarding National Weighting

The MDGs are global in their scope. The poverty figures are for the total world population. The EU social indicators are Union-wide, now extended to 25 countries with enlargement. Delors talked about 50 million people in Europe being in poverty. At the same time, we continue to attach weight to national identity, as revealed by the interest in country ranking. There is indeed a degree of ambivalence as to whether national identity is relevant to performance measurement. This ambivalence matters because countries differ so greatly in population size. Europe is moving to the construction of aggregate statistics: for example, total GDP for the euro zone. The large economies dominate such measures. The same applies to the poverty rate for the European Union, expressing the total number of people living in poverty as a percentage of the total EU population. Again, the large countries dominate such a figure. The performance of countries with populations of 10 million or less is not going to change greatly the overall rate. If an additional 10 percent of the Swedish population were suddenly to fall below the poverty line—a dramatic development for Sweden—the EU poverty rate would rise by less than a quarter of a percentage point. In contrast, if the UK were to reduce its poverty rate to that experienced in the 1970s, then the overall EU rate would fall by some 1.5 percentage points.

This consideration is becoming more pressing for the EU. Figure 4.2 shows the increasing concentration of the population of the EU with successive enlargements. It takes the form of a Lorenz-style diagram, where the EU member states are shown as a proportion of the total number of states along the horizontal (so that in EU25 each country counts as 4 percent), and their cumulative shares of total population are shown on the vertical. (The populations are those in 2002: source, European Commission, Statistics in Focus 20/2003.) If a third of the countries had a third of the total EU population, then the curve would follow the diagonal. But the smallest third of countries in fact have fewer than 5 percent of the total EU population, whereas the largest third of countries have 80 percent of the population. The concentration, in this sense, has increased. Taking the original EU6, the two largest countries would have 63 percent of the total population. Increased popula-

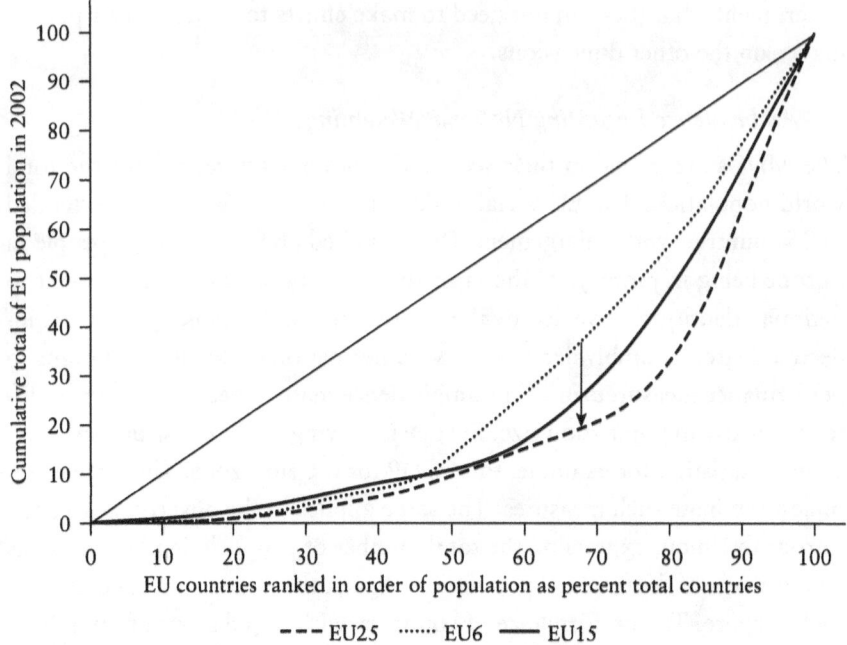

Figure 4.2. Concentration of EU Population by Country

tion concentration is going to raise more sharply the question as to whether we should give any additional weight to smaller countries when forming aggregate measures.

For the world as a whole, the populations of China (1.3 billion) and India (1 billion) are such that the experience of these two countries dominates the world indicators. Whether or not progress is made on the MDGs depends crucially on what happens in these two countries. But we still feel uncomfortable about in effect ignoring a large number of small countries.

Conclusions: Consciousness Raising

The adoption of EU social indicators and the MDGs represents a considerable political success for multilateral cooperation. The success is in part due to the contributions of social scientists. It is, however, the role of social science to be eternally critical, and the success in raising consciousness has brought also serious questions about the underlying concepts of social well-being, about this approach to multidimensionality, and about national weighting.

THE PROBLEMATIC RELATION WITH POLICY

Social indicators have played a significant role in raising the priority attached to poverty and social issues. The next step is to tackle the question, posed by Robert Eriksson at the symposium, as to the relation between social indicators and policy. Should researchers seek to link the indicators explicitly with policy? Should the EU member states have accepted the proposal of the commission to set an EU target for the halving of poverty? Should donor countries use the MDG indicators when allocating official development assistance?

National Performance Indicators

A key feature linking the EU and MDG processes is that they are international. Much of the literature relates, however, to the relation between indicators and policy at the national level, where the central government delegates policy choice to agencies, whose performance is to be judged according to specified indicators. In the macroeconomic context, for instance, governments have established independent central banks with a mandate to set interest policy to achieve an inflation target.

As noted in the Introduction, there is a parallel with the—now widely derided—resource allocation process in the Soviet economy. Under this process, Soviet managers had considerable freedom of action in achieving their specified (Plan) objectives and enterprises received bonuses once the output plan was fulfilled. Gregory and Stuart, in a textbook published just before the system ended (1989), described the strategies adopted by managers: "First, managers can . . . attempt to secure 'easy' targets. . . . Second, managers can emphasise what is important (in terms of their rewards) and neglect or ignore other areas. . . . Third, managers can seek 'safety' " (Gregory and Stuart 1989: 194). At a theoretical level, there was a literature on the determination of bonus schemes under central planning (for example, Merrett 1964) and on the optimum tautness of plans (for example, Portes 1969, and Keren 1972). It was recognized that targets must be set to induce greater exertion but not be so high powered that they distort too much the allocation of effort toward the targeted dimension. Moreover, the design of targets had to be seen as a dynamic process, new targets being set in the light of achieved performance. There is a potential ratchet effect.

The more recent, and rather separate, economic literature on principal/

agent relationships in private organizations has examined in depth the implications of the principal possessing only imperfect information about the possibilities open to the agent and the level of effort supplied (hidden information and hidden actions). For example, Milgrom and Roberts (1992: 221) describe the "Incentive Intensity Principle," according to which the optimal intensity of incentives depends positively on incremental profits created by additional effort, the precision with which the desired activities are assessed, the risk tolerance of the agent, and the responsiveness of the agent to incentives. The parallel with government organization is not exact, but lessons can be drawn (Tirole 1994). To the extent, for example, that outcomes are less precisely measured than profits, this may point to lower powered incentives in the public sphere.

International Context

What can be concluded about the more complex international situation? The first obvious point is that the parallel is at best partial. The principal does not have a hierarchical relation, with a principal setting objectives for the agent. In the case of the EU, the situation is symmetric where member states are setting indicators (and possibly targets) for themselves. In the global case, there is an asymmetry between rich and poor countries, but the principals are again setting objectives for themselves.

The principal agent relation is most clear if the relationship between donor and recipient countries is considered. A number of donor countries have put achievement of the MDGs at the center of their policy making. This influences their policy toward official development assistance (ODA). Suppose that donors in effect offer a "reward" structure, inviting recipient countries to specify a relation between ODA and progress toward the MDGs, where this relation embodies the effects of both ODA and domestic development effort. For example, a country may say that $10 million can be expected to bring about x million reduction in the number of people living below $1 a day. Donors then determine the volume and allocation of ODA. (As formulated, the problem is a dynamic one, but the iterative nature is not examined here.)

What lessons can be learned from the experience of planning and from the principal/agent literature? A key aspect is multiple dimensions. The principal/agent literature has examined the design of incentives where there are multiple tasks (Holmström and Milgrom 1991). If different agents responsible were for different dimensions, then there would be an argument for making the incentives more high powered where the goals are better measured. However, where an agency is pursuing multiple objectives, the power of incentives may have to be reduced for well-measured dimensions to avoid them dominating less precisely measured goals (Dixit 1996: 96). If ODA is tied strongly to poverty reduction, then this goal may displace the less precisely defined environmental concerns. This consideration points to less "targeted" allocations of ODA.

The form of the indicators is important here. Poverty is not only more precisely defined, but also is measured in Tables 4.1 and 4.2 in a way that accentuates the concentration of ODA. With a head-count measure, there is no recorded gain from an increase in household resources until that household crosses the poverty line. At a country level, there may therefore be a higher payoff in terms of the MDGs from targeting aid to those countries with large numbers of people close to the poverty line. Aid to India may make a larger contribution to reaching the MDG for poverty than aid to Africa. While the head count may have merits in terms of raising consciousness, it does not seem satisfactory as a link to policy formation. It would be preferable to use an indicator that reflects the extent of poverty shortfall, as proposed by Sen (1976).

Multilateral Agreements on Indicators and Targets

In the symmetric case, where a group of peer countries set themselves joint targets, the parallel is less close. Indeed, why should the EU member states adopt a set of common indicators to assess performance and contemplate setting EU targets? Why should countries set themselves targets for development? An important part of the answer must be commitment. Governments, recognizing their limited tenure, are keen to commit their successors; governments, recognizing their own frailties, are disposed to committing themselves not to deviate in the face of changed circumstances. Both Madame de Pompadour ("après nous le déluge") and Ulysses (bound to the mast) come into play. It would be difficult for a country to withdraw from the Millennium Development commitment. Rewriting the Lisbon agreement would require the agreement of a substantial majority of EU heads of state and government. There are also issues of credibility. In Atkinson (1996), I have argued that, in electoral competition, it may be in the interests of the more conservative party to commit itself to a poverty target, because it increases the credibility of a promise not to move too far away from redistributive policies.

Many of the same incentive issues, however, apply in this case. The choice of indicators must take account of their manipulability. Again head count does not seem a good option. Although figures for the numbers below a specified line are simple to explain, if employed as a target, they may well, as just shown, cause resources to be concentrated. A government can achieve its target of a percentage reduction in the poverty count by concentrating its policies on those within striking distance of the poverty line and ignoring the poorest. However, the risk of manipulation can be reduced if the publication of the indicators is accompanied by a reasoned account of the underlying policies and their wider implications. In the UK, I have argued (Atkinson 1996) that, parallel to the *Inflation Report* published by the Bank of England when reporting on its inflation performance, there should be a "Poverty Report," containing a commentary on the relation between the observed changes and policy action. The EU national action plans on social inclusion can perform this function.

The parallel with the incentive literature raises the question of absolute versus relative performance. Should performance be judged by an ideal standard, such as the elimination of poverty, or by reference to what has been actually achieved? Many remuneration schemes take the form of rank-order tournaments (Lazear and Rosen 1981), and the same can be applied to social indicators, when distance from the best-performing country is measured. It has been proposed, for example, that EU member states be set the target of closing the gap on the best three performing countries (for a discussion of possible approaches to target setting in the EU, see Atkinson et al. 2004). In the case of the MDGs, the goals are in effect a mixture. Universal primary education is an absolute goal (and has broadly been achieved in OECD countries). Reducing child mortality has implicitly the goal of reducing mortality to Western levels. In studies of remuneration, there are some grounds for supposing that rank-order measures have advantages when there is greater environmental uncertainty, common to all, about the determination of outcomes (Nalebuff and Stiglitz 1983), and it would be interesting to know whether this measurement carries over to the present context. If we are uncertain about the link between medical care and longevity, and about the upper limit to human life, is this grounds for adopting a target of matching best practice?

Conclusions: The Problematic Relation with Policy

In describing the relationship between indicators and policy making as "problematic," I am not suggesting that indicators should not be linked to policy. Rather, I am suggesting that the relationship is far from straightforward and raises a number of questions. Experience in other contexts with indicators and targets provides some clues as to the answers; investigators can learn from the literatures on the theory of the democratic process (Johansson 1990) and on economic incentives. There is serious work to be done.

THE CHALLENGE OF MEASURING PROGRESS

Politicians are preoccupied with change, and it is therefore inevitable that they will focus attention on the improvements recorded in the social indicators adopted by the EU and underlying the Millennium Development Goals. Each year in Europe the European Commission has to report on progress according to the agreed indicators, and this report will receive particular attention in the *Joint Reports on Social Inclusion*. Each year the UN Secretary General has to prepare a report on progress made toward implementing the Millennium Declaration.

Academic researchers have similarly stressed change and the time dimension. Their concerns have several elements, as is well brought out in the comments by Erikson on the indicators proposed by Atkinson et al. (2002): "The time period covered by the various indicators should be further considered. A given indicator may attain the same value when most people are exposed to an adverse condition during a short period as when a few people are exposed almost permanently. . . . It would also be informative if more emphasis were placed on the measurement of individual change. This would allow circumvention of some of the problems related to potential systematic differences between nations. Furthermore, change and non-change in adverse conditions are important factors per se, and the measurement of individual change allows investigation of not only net change but also gross change" (Erikson 2002: 70–71). As this quotation indicates, several related but different questions are raised about the treatment of time. How should investigators measure the permanent, as opposed to transitory, status of individuals? How should they measure change in individual status? How should they measure change in the status of the population? Here I consider only one: the implications of a focus on change for the design of indicators.

Different Indicators for Level and Change

To this point, I have assumed that, to each of the concerns, there corresponds a single, if imperfect, indicator. As soon, however, as an investigator contemplates measuring change, it becomes apparent that he or she may want to apply different (also imperfect) measures, playing to their relative strengths. Suppose that you were offered the choice between a watch that started off at the right time but randomly gained or lost an hour each day and a watch that kept perfect time but which was set initially to a random hour. If you wanted to know the time next day, then you would choose the first watch, being sure that the error would not exceed one hour. If you wanted to know how long you had slept, you would choose the second watch.

In the measurement of poverty, we should like, as indicated in the quotation from Erikson (2002), to identify the proportion of the population for whom it is a sustained, rather than purely transitory, phenomenon. Panel surveys have now made this feasible. Data from the European Community Household panel potentially covering some eight years gives a closer to permanent economic status by averaging data over several years. Those poor in three out of four years are more likely to be permanently poor than those who are below the poverty line in one or two out of the four years. But the more that the data are aggregated over time, the less that can be said about changes over time. A kind of Heisenberg uncertainty principle is in operation. The more sure that a household is in poverty (because their status is measured over more years), the less certain about it is whether or not their status has changed (because more years are needed to make the comparison).

There may, therefore, be reasons to take a different indicator to measure change over time from that employed to establish the base situation. For example, researchers may employ in the base year an indicator combining information on both income and direct indicators of deprivation, as in the "consistent poverty" measure employed in Ireland (National Anti-Poverty Strategy 1997), but use only deprivation indicators when measuring change over time (if they are assumed to be less subject to transitory variation). In measuring global poverty, investigators may use a purchasing power adjustment to establish the base poverty line across countries, but measure the change over time applying the national price changes separately in each country. It should be noted that such a procedure runs the risk of generating intransitivities that are revealed by a subsequent repeat of the base calculation. The national poverty line of year T indexed by the rate of inflation up to year $(T + t)$ may differ from the poverty line obtained by a new poverty line calculation for the year $(T + t)$. The cumulation of measured changes may not give the same result as the new baseline. Because the indicator targets typically have a limited horizon, this risk of intransitivity may be acceptable, but it needs to be recognized.

Timeliness: The Role of Input Indicators and Policy Modeling

The indicators employed by the EU and in assessing the MDGs differ in their degree of currency. Employment figures in EU countries typically relate to recent period, but other indicators can lag seriously. In 2003, the EU assessed progress toward poverty reduction on the basis of data at least three years out of date. The MDGs use indicators that depend on surveys where the results take time to be assembled, and which are, in many cases, only conducted at intervals or on population censuses that generate results typically at long intervals.

Timeliness matters particularly when measuring change. In its communication to the Spring 2002 European Council in Barcelona, the European Commission proposed that the European Council should set the target of halving the poverty rate to 9 percent by 2010. At that time, the latest information on income poverty for the EU member states as a whole related to 1997. Policy makers contemplating the implications of setting a target could reasonably have asked what progress has been made between 1997 and 2002. The annual reports of the UN Secretary General on progress toward the MDGs cannot repeat simply the figures underlying their launch.

The need for timely measures may mean that researchers have to look at other indicators, because they often have information about inputs well in advance of output indicators. In particular, it is here that input indicators may have a role to play. In some cases the change in a policy variable may be a valid instrument to forecast changes in the risk of poverty. For example, an increase in development aid may be taken as a sign that more resources are being channeled into development. Such use should be carefully justified. Any policy effort indicator would need to be shown to be closely related to outcomes. To take an example, investigators may be concerned about the number of people in inadequate housing, and the number of new houses built is a relevant input indicator, but investigators cannot be sure a priori that these houses are going to the people in need: that link would need to be studied empirically.

Here policy modeling can play a valuable role. Suppose that a government has improved family benefits. The impact on the poor depends on the distribution of the benefits, the level of take-up, and on the interaction with other parts of the system: for example, increases in one transfer benefit may lead to a withdrawal of other benefits. Such interactions occur where means-tested safety net benefits are withdrawn as other sources of income are improved. In the absence of current information on policy outcomes, it may be possible to simulate the effect of policy changes using tax benefit models. Models such as EUROMOD (see, for example, Immervoll et al. 2001) provide an estimate of the impact of policy unaffected by changes in other variables, and a time series of such simulated effects could then be used as an input into forecasting equations for the poverty rate.

CONCLUSION: WAYS FORWARD AND HARD QUESTIONS

The review in this chapter of social indicators and their policy role has attempted to be constructively critical. Among the positive conclusions are:

1. A clear separation of outputs and inputs—social indicators to be concerned with outcomes, but recognizing that input measures may have a role in assessing the prospect for progress.

2. The need for indicators to change smoothly with policy variables, avoiding discrete switches in policies and overpowerful incentives.

3. The role of a reasoned account of policy choices, to accompany social indicators, as in a poverty report, to avoid overconcentration on the selected indicators.

4. Recognition that the indicators chosen to measure the extent of a problem may not be the best indicators of change over time, even at the risk of generating possible intransitivities.

It is also clear that hard questions remain. The choice of social indicators challenges social scientists to define more precisely, and in an implementable way, the underlying definition of social welfare. Aggregation across different dimensions presents a trade-off between unwieldy amounts of information and implicit judgments of value. There is ambivalence concerning national weighting. The role of targets as a commitment device needs elaboration. What is the optimum degree of "tautness" when setting targets? Much remains to be done.

Notes

1. The paper reflects on work on social indicators undertaken with Bea Cantillon, Eric Marlier, and Brian Nolan, and I would like to thank them for the stimulus provided by this collaboration. I am most grateful to the commentators, Johan Fritzell and Inga Persson, and to the participants in the Sigtuna Symposium, for their helpful remarks. I thank Sten Johansson for making available a copy of his paper (1990) in English. Laurens Cherchye, Eric Marlier, and Wim Moesen all provided valuable comments on a previous draft, which have led to significant improvements. None of the above is however to be held responsible for the views expressed.

2. After sending the first version of this paper to Johan Fritzell, I learned that he had preceded me in having the same idea—see Fritzell (2003).

References

Anand, S. and Sen, A. K. 1997. Concepts of Human Development and Poverty: A Multidimensional Perspective, Human Development Papers, United Nations Development Programme, New York.

Atkinson, A. B. 1996. Promise and Performance: Why We Need an Official Poverty Report. In P. Barker (ed.), *Living as Equals*. Oxford: Oxford University Press.

Atkinson, A. B. 2003. Multidimensional Deprivation: Contrasting Social Welfare and Counting Approaches. *Journal of Economic Inequality* 1: 51–65.

Atkinson, A. B., Cantillon, B., Marlier, E., and Nolan, B. 2002. *Social Indicators: The EU and Social Inclusion*. Oxford: Oxford University Press.

Atkinson, A. B., Marlier, E., and Nolan, B. 2004. Indicators and Targets for Social Inclusion in the European Union. *Journal of Common Market Studies*.

Chen, S., and Ravallion, M. 2001. How Did the World's Poorest Fare in the 1990s? *Review of Income and Wealth* 47: 283–300.

Cherchye, L., Moesen, W., and Van Puyenbroeck, T. 2003. Legitimately Diverse, Yet Comparable: On Synthesising Social Inclusion Performance in the EU. Centre for Economic Studies Discussion Paper 03.01, Katholieke Universiteit Leuven.

Dixit, A. K. 1996. *The Making of Economic Policy*. Cambridge: MIT Press.

Erikson, R. 1974. Welfare as a Planning Goal. *Acta Sociologica* 17: 273–88.

Erikson, R. 1993. Descriptions of Inequality: The Swedish Approach to Welfare Research. In M. C. Nussbaum and A. Sen (eds.), *The Quality of Life*. Oxford: Clarendon.

Erikson, R. 2002. Social Indicators for the European Union: Comments. *Politica economica* 17: 69–73.

Erikson, R. and Tåhlin, M. 1987. Coexistence of Welfare Problems. In R. Erikson and R. Åberg (eds.), *Welfare in Transition*. Oxford: Clarendon.

European Commission. 1985. On Specific Community Action to Combat Poverty (Council Decision of 19 December 1984). 85/8/EEC, *Official Journal of the EEC*, 2/24.

European Commission. 2002. *Joint Report on Social Inclusion, Communication from the Commission*, COM (2001) 565 final.

European Commission. 2003. First Results of the Demographic Data Collection for 2002 in Europe. *Statistics in Focus* No. 2.

Fritzell, J. 2003. The Swedish Multidimensional Approach to the Study of Welfare—Theoretical Foundation and Empirical Applications. Presented at seminar, Havana, April 2–4, 2003.

Gregory, P. R. and Stuart, R. C. 1989. *Comparative Economic Systems*, 3rd ed. Boston: Houghton Mifflin.

Hagenaars, A., de Vos, K., and Zaidi, A. 1994. *Poverty Statistics in the Late 1980s*. Luxembourg: Eurostat.

Holmström, B. and Milgrom, P. 1991. Multitask Principal-Agent Analysis: Incentive Contracts, Asset Ownership, and Job Design. *Journal of Law, Economics, and Organization* 7: 24–51.

Immervoll, H., Sutherland, H., and de Vos, K. 2001. Reducing Child Poverty in the European Union: The Role of Child Benefits. In K. Vleminckx and T. M. Smeeding (eds.), *Child Well-Being, Child Poverty and Child Policy in Modern Nations*. Bristol: Policy Press.

Johansson, S. 1990 The Epistemology of the Democratic Process. *Swedish Institute for Social Research*, Stockholm University.

Keren, M. 1972. On the Tautness of Plans. *Review of Economic Studies* 39: 469–486.

Lazear, E. P. and Rosen, S. 1981. Rank-Order Tournaments as Optimum Labor Contracts. *Journal of Political Economy* 89: 841–64.

Merrett, S. 1964. Capital, Profit and Bonus in Soviet Industry. *Economica* 31: 401–407.

Milgrom, P. and Roberts, J. 1992. *Economics, Organization and Management*. Englewood Cliffs, N.J.: Prentice Hall.

Nalebuff, B. J. and Stiglitz, J. E. 1983. Prizes and Incentives: Towards a General Theory of Compensation and Competition. *Bell Journal of Economics* 14: 21–43.

National Anti-Poverty Strategy. 1997. *Sharing in Progress*, Stationery Office, Dublin.

Nolan, B. 1999. Targeting Poverty. *New Economy* 6: 44–49.

Portes, R. D. 1969. The Enterprise under Central Planning. *Review of Economic Studies* 36: 197–212.

Sen, A. K. 1976. Poverty: An Ordinal Approach to Measurement. *Econometrica* 44: 219–31.

Social Protection Committee. 2001. Report from the Chairman to the SPC, Brussels.

Social Protection Committee. 2003. Common Outline for the 2003/2005 NAPs/ inclusion, Brussels.

Tirole, J. 1994. The Internal Organization of Government. *Oxford Economic Papers* 46: 1–29.

UNDP. 1990. *Human Development Report 1990*. Oxford: Oxford University Press.

U.S. Department of Health, Education, and Welfare. 1969. *Toward a Social Report*. Washington, D.C.: U.S. Government Printing Office.

World Bank. 1990. *World Development Report 1990: Poverty*. Oxford: Oxford University Press.

World Bank. 2001. *World Development Report 2000/2001 Attacking Poverty*. Oxford: Oxford University Press.

CHAPTER FIVE

Family Structure, Gender Roles, and Social Inequality

Annemette Sørensen

The last fifty years have witnessed changes in household and family structure and in women's economic roles in all of the rich industrialized countries.[1] Divorce rates are high, cohabitation common, many children experience an unstable family life while growing up, many children do not live with or have much contact with their father, and childbearing outside marriage is as high as it has ever been. Families have also become smaller, marriages occur later in life, and children are born to parents who are considerably older than was the case forty years ago. Finally, women have gained a great deal of economic power; their earnings capacity is high by historical standards, labor force participation rates are high also for married women, and women's earnings are an increasingly important foundation for a household's standard of living. These demographic changes, often referred to as the Second Demographic Transition (Lestaeghe 1995), amount to profound changes in the economic foundations of marriage, in gender relations within families, in the stability of families and households, and in children's family lives. In this chapter, I ask how these changes may have affected the stratification system.[2]

The family plays a role in the stratification system in three ways: (1) the family is a redistributive unit in the sense that its members to a large extent pool and share resources intragenerationally as well as across generations; (2) the family exerts some control and influence over its members, making families a source for constraints or encouragements of the achievements of individual family members; and (3) it is an important source for the maintenance of inequality, that is for the transmission of advantage and disadvantage across generations.

It has been clear for several decades that women's new economic roles had important consequences for the family as an economic and social unit. As a result, the conventional way of studying social mobility faced a major challenge because key assumptions seemed no longer to be tenable. Specifically, the assumption that the family's class position can be gauged by the class position of the male head of the household came under fire (Acker 1973; Crompton and Mann 1986; Goldthorpe 1983; Erikson 1984; Sørensen 1994; Szelényi 2001). As long as most married women were not employed outside the home, this assumption presumably was quite unproblematic, although it is unknown if conclusions about intergenerational mobility would have been affected by the inclusion of female-headed households in mobility studies. During the 1970s, when married women's employment became more common, although for many intermittent, the old assumption became less credible, and the empirical changes in women's lives represented a serious challenge to the conventional empirical practice. In John Goldthorpe's debate with feminist scholars in the 1980s, he vigorously rejected the suggestion that when a wife was employed, her occupation should in some manner be taken into account when assessing the family's class position (Goldthorpe 1983), arguing that it was *because* of women's weak position in the labor market and their continuing dependence on a spouse that it should be the husband's position that determined a family's class position.[3]

Another argument used against taking women's labor market position into account was that by doing so, too much mobility would be generated, because the family's class position would change every time the wife moved in and out of the labor force. A so-called joint classification measure would thus "greatly accentuate problems of defining class boundaries and tend to produce rates of class mobility that we would regard as spuriously high" (Erikson and Goldthorpe 1992: 238). As I have noted elsewhere, this is a curious criticism. If a family's class position in fact depends on the work position of both husband and wife, then "the mobility that is 'introduced' by the joint classification measure is true class mobility, and, as such may have serious consequences for the stability of classes and the formation of class consciousness and class action" (Sørensen 1994: 37). Mobility will also be increased by the inclusion of female-headed households in mobility research, because most female-headed households result from the dissolutions of male-headed households due to divorce. It then should be evident, that it is a distinct *possibility* that one of the consequences of the Second Demographic

Transition has been to *increase* the mobility that members of a family or household experience over their lifetime, simply because there has been an increase in the incidence of events with the potential to change a household's life conditions (DiPrete 2002).

Several other potential consequences of the new demographic regime arise for the stratification system. In this chapter, I focus on three of them:

1. To what extent can recent increases in family and household inequality be attributed to changes in family structure and women's earnings?

2. To what extent have children's life chances been affected by changes in family forms and gender roles and by the change in family and household inequality, specifically have they led to greater inequality among children?

3. Has the family's ability to transmit advantage to their children been weakened, in other words has the mobility regime become more fluid, or is it rather the case that the link between social origins and destinations has become stronger?

I focus my examination of the empirical literature on the United States. There are two reasons for doing so: (1) This is arguably where most of the relevant research has been done, although the empirical evidence for other countries is mounting; and (2) the consequences of many of the changes in family structure and gender roles will most likely be different in different countries, because public policy and the welfare state are important mediating factors (DiPrete 2002). I therefore attempt to provide answers for the case of the United States, which probably can be seen as a worst case scenario, and then conclude the chapter with a discussion of the factors that would lead to different expectations for the situation in other countries.[4]

INEQUALITY IN THE DISTRIBUTION OF FAMILY AND HOUSEHOLD INCOME

> The most rapid increases in work have been among women in families with higher incomes. Increases in earnings among wives in high-income families increase family income inequality. Thurow has suggested that although wives' earnings were once a factor leading to an equalization of family incomes, they are now "becoming a course of family inequality."
>
> —Danziger 1980: 3

It is well known that inequality in the distribution of family and household income in the United States has increased steadily from the mid-1970s, after a sustained decline after the end of World War II. The Gini coefficient for household income in the late 1960s varied around .390. In the mid-1970s household income inequality began to grow. In 1980, the Gini coefficient was .403; in 1990 it was .428 and in 2002 it reached .462 (De Navas-Walt et al. 2003: Table A4). The increase in household income inequality reflected three changes in the distribution: Some decline in the percentage of households having incomes below $25,000 (2002 dollars) from 38 percent in 1967 to 29 percent in 2002. Also relatively fewer households had incomes in the middle range (from $25,000 to $74,999), declining from 55 percent in 1967 to 46 percent in 2002. The big change was observed in the high income category, $75,000 and above. In 1967, only 8 percent of households had incomes of this magnitude, by 1990 it had increased to 19 percent, and in 2002 fully one-quarter of American households had incomes exceeding $75,000 (De Navas-Walt et al. 2003: Table A1).[5]

Looking only at family households, the trends in overall income inequality are the same as for all households, with one important exception. Instead of a decline in the percentage of households with low incomes, the percentage of family households with low incomes increased somewhat between the mid-1970s and the late 1990s (Levy 1997: 40–41), an increase that likely has not been reversed since then.

Three reasons for the increase in inequality between households are usually cited, namely changes in the mix of different household types; changes in married women's labor supply and earnings capacity, including an increase in the correlation between husbands' and wives' earnings (Cancian and Reed 1999); and increases in the inequality of individual earnings (Levy 1997). There is consensus in recent research that changes in household composition and size have contributed to the increase in inequality, although there are disagreements on the role played by changes in women's earnings. One study concluded that about two-fifths of the increase in income inequality between households could be attributed to changes in the mix of households (single persons, one-parent families, two-parent families) between 1969 and 1989, while changes in wages and other sources of income, including women's earnings, accounted for the remaining two-fifths of the increase (Ryscavage et al. 1992). It seems reasonable to infer that changes in the mix of families toward more families headed by a single person, in particular a woman, and fewer husband–wife families would have a similar effect on the distribution of family income (Levy 1997). Another study concluded that "trends in earnings inequality among working men and in the correlation between women's earnings and family income explain more than half of the increase in overall inequality since 1979. A significant part of the remaining increase is attributable to trends in family composition" (Karoly and Burtless 1995: 401). The conclusions regarding the effects of women's earnings have been challenged in a recent study that explicitly compared the observed changes in inequality with those that would have been obtained if there had been no change in women's earnings and in the within-household correlation between men's and women's earnings (Cancian and Reed 1999). Using this conclusion as the counterfactual, the study found that "despite the rising correlation between husbands' and wives' earnings, changes in women's earnings did not explain a substantial portion of the increase in family income inequality" (Cancian and Reed 1999: 173). Instead, changes in men's earnings had played a significant role in this increase.

It seems reasonable to conclude that the increase of single-mother households as well as the growth in single-person households have been one of the sources of change in the distribution of family and household income in the United States. It is less clear whether the increase in women's earnings has played a decisive role, although all studies show that the increase in inequality in American men's earnings has been an important source.

INEQUALITY IN CHILDREN'S ATTAINMENTS

> Family life has important bearing on occupational life. Broken families spell lower occupational achievements for both the children and the husband, though it is not clear whether the husband's less successful career is a consequence of the marriage break-up or helps to precipitate it.
> —Blau and Duncan 1967: 410

> [T]he independent influence of mother's socioeconomic status may lead to an accumulation of educational advantages and disadvantages in subsequent generations, possibly reducing the intergenerational mobility of families.
> —Kalmijn 1994: 257

> The decline of fatherhood and of marriage cuts at the heart of the kind of environment considered ideal for child rearing.
> —Popenoe 1996: 14

There is by now a large literature on the effects of parental divorce and family structure on children's life chances. Two strands of this research are of special interest here, namely studies of the effects on children's economic status and their educational and occupational attainment.

Family structure is a very important determinant of children's risk of living in poverty. A study based on data from 1994 found that the overall poverty rate among children was 24 percent, while more than half of children lived in prosperous families, defined as families with incomes greater than twice the poverty cutoff. Among children in married-couple families almost 13 percent lived in poverty, while more than half of children (55 percent) in female-headed families did so. Prosperity rates were relatively high among children in married-couple families at 65 percent, while only one in five of children in female-headed families were this well off.

Data from 2001 suggest that the situation had improved somewhat by then, although the stark difference between two-parent families and single-mother families persisted. In 2001, the overall poverty rate among children was 16 percent. For children in married-couple families it was 8 percent, and in single-mother families almost five times as high at 39 percent (Moore and Redd 2002).

Adding to the dismal picture of the economic well-being of children living in mother-headed families, such children not only run a high risk of living in poverty but many of them live in extreme poverty. In their study of children's economic well-being in rich societies, Rainwater and Smeeding (2003), using data from the 1990s, found that in the United States, fully 30 percent of children in single-mother families lived in extreme poverty, that is in households with an equivalent income below one-third of the median equivalent household income. Twenty-two percent lived in poor families with incomes between one-third and one-half the median household income, and 17 percent in near poor families with incomes below two-thirds of the median equivalent household income. This means in turn that barely a third (31 percent) of the children in single-mother households live in families with average or higher than average incomes. In contrast, more than three-quarters (78 percent) of children in two-parent households live in families with average and higher than average incomes (Rainwater and Smeeding 2003).

There is no doubt that American children's economic status is severely affected by the type of family in which they live. The structure of children's families are in turn determined by their parents' choices to divorce or to have children outside marriage. I must conclude, then, that one of the clear consequences of high divorce rates and increasing proportion of children being born out of wedlock has been a deterioration of American children's economic circumstances.

Growing Up with a Single Parent

Let's now turn the attention to how children's attainment might have been affected by their parents' divorce or by growing up with a single parent. A recent review of American research concluded that children of divorce "score significantly lower on measures of academic achievement, conduct, psychological adjustment, self concept, and social relations" (Amato 2001: 355), and that children who grew up in a single-parent household or with a stepparent were less likely to complete high school and college, less likely to find stable employment in young adulthood, and more likely to bear children outside marriage (McLanahan and Sandefur 1994). Some studies also suggest that such children were more likely to have poor mental health in adulthood, although a majority of children of divorce did not experience poor mental health (Cherlin et al. 1998). All these studies also find that much of the effect of parental divorce and family structure can be accounted for by the fact that the socioeconomic position of families depends so strongly on the structure of the family.

It is probably fair to characterize these findings as the "new consensus" about these matters, but it is important to point out, as Biblarz and Raftery (1999) note, that not all studies find these negative effects of divorce and family structure. For example, in an examination of census data from 1990, Mare (1995) reports few and weak effects on school transitions of living in a single-mother or single-father family, compared with two parents. The discrepancy between studies can have many sources, but two stand out as being most important: (1) studies have been done at different time points opening the possibility that discrepant findings reflect real changes over time in the effects of family structure and parental divorce, and (2) most studies present results for the net effects of family structure, but the variables that are controlled for vary.

In a very careful study, using four different datasets covering the period 1962 to 1996, Biblarz and Raftery (1999) found that there had been no change over time in the effect of family structure on children's educational and occupational attainment. Models specifying a constant effect over time provided the better fit. Not surprisingly, they also found that conclusions indeed depended on the variables included in the model. For example, if the model includes a control for family size, the effect of living with mother alone is enhanced, although controls for socioeconomic status make the effect smaller and at times nonsignificant. It is therefore a considerable service for the research community that the authors specify a series of identical models for different points in time, thereby making it possible to describe the conditions under which effects of family structure are smaller or larger.

Several of the conclusions from this study are of interest here. First, children growing up in two-parent families had significantly higher occupational and educational attainments than did children growing up in single-parent and stepfather families. This was the case throughout the almost four decades spanned by the studies. The effects on occupational attainment were modest ranging between 2.1 and 4.7 points for the effects of growing up in a mother-headed family, for example. In the two early studies this effect was smaller than the effect if growing up in a household where the household head was not employed. In the two latter studies, the effect of family structure was about the same as having a household head that was not employed. So the effects on current socioeconomic status (SEI) are relatively modest. In addition, it should be noted that the explained variance in the basic model including family structure variables and race is very low, ranging from 2 to 7 percent. The second important finding is that, once the family's socioeconomic position[6] was taken into account, the difference between two-parent and single-mother families became insignificant, while the negative effects of the other two nontraditional family types persisted. In other words, if single-mother families were as likely to be headed by an employed woman with an occupational status similar to the male head of two-parent families, then children in these two family types would fare equally well, while equalizing socioeconomic conditions for the other types of families would have no such effect.

The results with respect to educational attainment, measured as years of schooling, were very similar to the results for socioeconomic status. However, the return to education in the form of occupational status was found to be smaller for children living in alternative family types. This means that such children not only on average received less schooling, they also benefited less from the schooling they did receive. Children from two-parent families gained 4 SEI points for each additional year of schooling, children from single-mother and single-father families gained 3.5 SEI points and children from stepfather families gained 3 points per additional year of schooling.

This study then confirmed that in the United States there are some negative consequences for children's life chances of their parent's divorce and remarriage or for a mother to give birth to a child out of wedlock.[7] It also confirmed that socioeconomic conditions can account for differences between children in two-parent families and in mother-headed families. This clearly is an important finding pointing to the possibility that an alleviation of the economic risks associated with single motherhood will go a long way toward removing achievement barriers for children in these families. It is important to point out, however, that American children in mother-headed families do live under socioeconomic circumstances that lower their educational and occupational attainment, and that this is a direct consequence of family structure. The differences between two-parent families and other types of nontraditional families (single-father and stepfather families) are not accounted for by differences in socioeconomic standing, and it remains a matter of debate why these family types seem to present barriers to children's attainment.

Given the relatively modest size of the effects of family structure, investigators might just shrug them off as of being no real importance. I do not think this is a warranted conclusion. About half of all children in the United States are expected to live for some time in a single-parent household before reaching adulthood, and about one in three children will experience living with a stepparent (Amato 2000: 1270). These statistics suggest that a substantial portion of American children are presented with additional achievement barriers that their friends growing up in two-parent families do not confront.[8]

Do these results suggest that changes in family structure have contributed to an increase in inequality among children with respect to educational and occupational attainment? Or to put it differently, would the achievements of children not living with their two parents have been better, had their parents not divorced, remarried, or had a child out of wedlock (Ni-Bhrolcháin 2001)? The answer to this question depends on whether the associations, that clearly are present, are causal effects. There is a good deal of disagreement about this. Clearly, if an argument can be sustained for the family structure effects to be purely the result of selection on say weak parenting skills, high levels of conflict between parents, or children having difficulties of one type or another, then effects that look like effects of family structure in fact are due to preexisting conditions that would have had negative effects on the children even if the parents had lived as a two-parent family (e.g., Gähler 1998; Jekielek 1998). Longitudinal studies do suggest, however, that family structure effects remain, even after careful controls for preexisting factors (e.g., Cherlin et al. 1998; Hanson 1999; McLanahan and Sandefur 1994). It is clear that not all of the observed differences between two-parent and other types of families can be attributed to the effects of divorce, remarriage, or single motherhood, and that it indeed may be to some children's advantage if their parents no longer live together. It is also clear that many children of divorce, single- and step-parenthood do well on a range of measures of child achievement and well-being outcomes (Cherlin 1999). At the same time, investigators should not ignore the fact that one of the clearest outcomes of divorce or single motherhood is that the child's socioeconomic circumstances are likely to be considerably worse than if the parents shared a household. This is a direct causal effect, and one, as shown earlier, that is likely to have adverse effects on children's schooling and subsequently on their occupational chances.

My reading of the American literature is that if most children grew up with their two biological parents, then the average educational and occupational attainment would be higher than what is observed today, and the variance would be lower. In other words, changes in children's family lives have made it more difficult for an increasing proportion of children to achieve as much as they would have were the likelihood that a child grows up with two parents the same as it were fifty years ago.

Mothers' Employment and Earnings

Another major change in children's lives has been that an increasing proportion of children have mothers who are employed throughout most of their childhood. This clearly has consequences for the economic situation of the family, and there is some evidence that the increase in women's labor supply and earnings capacity has been important for many American families' ability to maintain their living standards during times when many men have been experiencing slow growth and even decline in their wages (Levy 1997).

To the extent that children are adversely affected by poor economic circumstances in their family, the increase in mothers' earnings should have been beneficial for children.

There is also some evidence that the employed mother's educational and occupational attainment affect children's schooling as much as do their father's, and that these effects have been increasing over time (Kalmijn 1994). This finding is modified by the fact that children of non-working mothers did better educationally than children whose mothers were employed, unless the mother had a relatively high education and high status job. For children born in 1940, having a mother who was not employed increased the chances of graduating high school and college, although children whose mother held a high status job did almost as well. For the cohort born in 1960, things were a bit different. The chance of graduating high school was a bit smaller for children with mothers employed in low status jobs or jobs with average SEI scores, while mothers with a high status job and non-working mothers had children who almost all graduated from high school. For the transition to college and graduation from college, children whose mothers held low status or average status jobs were less likely to make the transition than were children whose mothers were not employed. But children whose mothers held high status jobs were considerably more likely to enter college (88 percent) and to graduate from college (70 percent).

The results of this study suggest that the influence of mother's employment and occupational status is considerable, but that it is largely children of mothers with high status jobs whose educational attainment is facilitated over and above the attainment of children of stay-at-home mothers. Because single mothers on average have lower educational and occupational attainment (Biblarz and Raftery 1999: Table 3), their employment may then be one of the factors contributing to the creation of barriers for their children, thus adding to the effect of their relatively low economic status.

It is difficult, given the relatively limited literature on the subject, to make strong conclusion about how mothers' employment and earnings have affected children's life chances. On the one hand, mothers' earnings constitute an increasingly important part of most families' income (Levy 1997; Sørensen 2004) and in that sense their new economic role should benefit children. On the other hand, if Kalmijn is right that only employment in high status jobs has a positive effect on children's educational attainment, then the positive effect of mother's earnings may be offset by the negative effect of their employment in jobs with lower status. My tentative conclusion is that the change in women's economic roles may have had little or no influence on children's educational attainment at the lower-to-middle level of mother's education and socioeconomic status, but that children whose mothers are well educated and holding high status jobs have gained an added benefit, which often will be added to the positive effects of an equally well-educated father with another high status job. The end result may then be that inequality among children in educational attainment may have increased somewhat due to the increase in the proportion of children with mothers with high status jobs.

Increasing Income Inequality and Children's Educational Attainment

As inequality in family incomes has increased, has that had any influence on the educational attainment of children? Specifically, has this widening of the gap between the poor and the well-off increased the association between social origin and children's educational attainment? This is what would be expected, if parents and children make schooling decisions as outlined in the theory of educational choice developed by Breen and Goldthorpe (1997). The theory posits that parents and children make schooling decisions that take into account three factors: the cost of remaining in school, the likelihood of success if the student stays in school, and the utility that children and their parents attach to a given schooling outcome. Of particular relevance here is the cost of remaining in school. Researchers should expect that more families will find it difficult to cover the costs of having their children stay in school, as more families live on lower incomes, but also that enrollment rates among children of well-off parents will have increased.[9] A recent analysis (Mayer 2001) does indeed find empirical support for such a change. She found that since the 1970s when inequality began to increase, college enrollment rates increased, but also that the inequality in educational attainment between rich and poor children increased: "A .02 increase in the Gini coefficient is associated with a reduction of .192 years in low-income children's schooling and an increase of .372 years in high-income children's schooling" (Mayer 2001: 22). In other words, the association between the family's social and economic position and children's educational attainment has increased as family income inequality has gone up.

Overall, it then seems reasonable to say that changes in family structure, women's roles, and in family income inequality probably have meant more inequality among children in educational attainment than there would have been if these changes had not taken place. Researchers should expect such differences to turn into more inequality in occupational attainment, given the increasing importance of education and especially a college degree in the American stratification system (Hout 1988; Levy 1997).

IS THERE MORE OR LESS OPENNESS IN THE INTERGENERATIONAL MOBILITY REGIME?

> [R]elative rates will be basically the same across all societies that have market economies and (at least) nuclear family systems, whatever stage of their industrial development may have reached; and thus, when examined over time within particular industrial societies, relative rates should reveal little change at all.
>
> —Erikson and Goldthorpe 1992: 24

The family is an important source for the perpetuation of inequality, simply because most parents see it in their interest and as their responsibility to encourage and help their offspring to achieve at least as much as they themselves have. The prevalence of an ideology of equal opportunity in American society represents societal forces working to limit the direct parental influence on their children's life chances, and there are indeed many opportunities to succeed that are not rooted in the family of origin (e.g., Blau and Duncan 1967). Those opportunities would appear to have become better over time. The influence of family background has gradually been reduced since Blau and Duncan did their study in 1962. Featherman and Hauser (1978) found that the effect of social origins on occupational destination had decreased between 1962 and 1973, and a study covering the period from 1972 to 1989 (Grusky and DiPrete 1990: 617) concluded that the "returns to class-based advantages" had been further eroded, a conclusion that is supported by Hout's study (1988) of intergenerational mobility for the same period. The question I am asking here is what the change in "returns to class-based advantages" would have been, had social science not seen the last fifty years of change in family structure and women's economic roles. Or to put it differently, is it so that two-parent families are better able to transmit advantage to their children than other family forms? The research reviewed in the previous section suggests that this is indeed the case. Does that then mean that as more children grow up under other circumstances, that society will grow more open, that is, one where the association between social origin and destination is weaker? Or will the opposite situation occur, where the correlation between where a person comes from and where he or she ends up is becoming stronger?

Family Structure and Social Mobility

Despite Blau and Duncan's (1967) interest in how growing up in an "intact family" affected the status attainment process of men, there is a rather limited literature on the effects of family disruption on social mobility. Important exceptions are three studies, two using data on intergenerational mobility from OCG II (Biblarz and Raftery 1993; Biblarz et al. 1997) and one, referred to earlier, using data from four different surveys covering the period 1962 to 1996 (Biblarz and Raftery 1999). The first study concluded that men from nonintact family backgrounds had a greater chance of ending up in low status occupations than in high status occupations. The differences were quite large. "Coming from a nonintact background increases the odds of ending up in the lowest socioeconomic stratum as against the highest by over fifty percent" (Biblarz and Raftery 1993: 105) for men with the same origin and race. This is, of course, consistent with results reported above of a negative effect of not growing up with both parents on the educational and occupational attainment of children. The study also found that "family disruption weakens intergenerational inheritance and resemblance, even after disruption's direct effects are taken into account" (Biblarz and Raftery 1993: 107). In other words, there was a significant net interaction between family structure and the origin-destination association.

Extending this study to differentiate between different types of "nonintact" families (Biblarz et al. 1997), the authors found that men from mother-headed families did as well as men from intact families, once differences in social origin had been taken into account, while it was men from father-headed and step-families that experienced a negative effect of family structure. This outcome then suggests that the original finding of an effect of nonintact family is an effect of single-father and step-families rather than an effect attributable to all nontraditional family types. The authors interpret these results to mean that what matters for children is to grow up close to their mother; indeed they say that "the farther alternative family structures take children away from mothers, the more the intergenerational transmission process breaks down" (Biblarz et al. 1997: 1333). These results, although not their interpretation, are very similar to the findings reported earlier, that once socioeconomic differences were taken into account, children from mother-headed families did as well educationally as children from two-parent families.

The results of the analyses of intergenerational mobility tables then suggest that the association between social origin and destination is weaker for all alternative family structures, suggesting that as fewer children grow up in two-parent families, the intergenerational mobility pattern would move in the direction of more openness. This is further supported by research using a status attainment approach (Biblarz and Raftery 1999). This study, which was discussed in detail above, found an interaction between social origin and alternative family forms on children's occupational attainment. The effect of social origin was stronger for children from two-parent families and weakest for children from stepfather families, with children from mother-headed and single-father families in between. Another way to interpret this is that family structure matters more for offspring from high status families, although there is virtually no difference for low status families. As the authors conclude, "sons from low socioeconomic origins tend to end up in low socioeconomic origins regardless of family type. Among children from the high end of origin SEI, differences in socioeconomic attainment across family types are substantial" (Biblarz and Raftery 1999: 351).

As fewer children grow up in two-parent families, social scientists should expect a more open intergenerational mobility regime, in the sense that parents at the higher end of the status hierarchy have more difficulty transmitting their advantaged position to their children if they do not bring up the children in a two-parent family. The effect of social origin on children's achievement will be weakened in the upper end of the status hierarchy, the fewer children grow up in two-parent families. Investigators should not forget, however, that nontraditional families with low socioeconomic resources on average lower the children's educational attainment, largely because of limited resources, and thus contributing to a greater association between social origin and educational attainment.

CONCLUDING DISCUSSION

I have attempted in this chapter to survey a dispersed literature to find answers to three questions about the possible influence on the American stratification system of the profound changes in family forms and gender roles during the last four to five decades. It seems to me that there is pretty good evidence in support of the notion that the increase in family and household income inequality to some extent can be attributed to changes in family and household structure, while the jury is still out on the extent to which women's increased earnings have played a significant role. I also think that research provides sufficient evidence for the claim that changes in family structure, in women's economic roles, and in family income inequality has meant more inequality among American children in educational attainment, and thus in subsequent occupational attainment, than there would have been had these changes not taken place. The intergenerational mobility regime may have become somewhat more universalistic as a result of the increasing proportion of children who do not grow up with both parents, because higher status single-parent or stepfamilies find it more difficult to pass on advantage to their children than do two-parent families.

I have purposefully limited my exploration so far to the United States. This decision was not rooted in the belief that the American case illustrates what investigators would find in other rich societies, but rather in the assumption that the consequences of the Second Demographic Transition might be very different in different societies. The next step is therefore to begin a discussion of the societal conditions and mechanisms that lie beneath such differences. In his insightful analysis of mobility regimes in Germany, Sweden, and the United States, DiPrete (2002) suggests that country differences in mobility regimes can be characterized "rather concisely in terms of rates of events and their consequences" (p. 299), where events refer to transitions that may have an effect on a household's socioeconomic position, such as a divorce or the loss of a job for one of the members of the household. He identifies Germany as a society with institutions that tend to inhibit the rate of such events (low divorce rates, employment protection), but also a society with substantial negative consequences of a divorce, for example. Sweden is an example of the opposite; events that may alter the household's socioeconomic standing occur frequently, but the welfare state provides a buffer, so that the consequences are relatively minor. Finally, the United States is similar to Sweden regarding the rate at which class-altering events occur, but quite different from Sweden with respect to the consequences of such events, with a welfare state that provides few and weak buffers. The combination of the rate of class-altering events and their consequences translates into substantial national differences in the probability of experiencing severe downward mobility as a result of a divorce or unemployment, with American men and women at considerably higher risk than German and Sweden men and women. There are also gender differences in all three countries, stemming primarily from the higher risk of downward mobility that women experience in connection with a divorce.

Although DiPrete's analysis focuses on life course mobility, the core ideas can be applied directly to the issues that have been the focus in this chapter. Assessing how the Second Demographic Transition has affected the stratification system in other countries, researchers first need to ask how much change there has been in children's family lives and in women's economic roles; and the second question to ask is what the socioeconomic consequences of these changes are. As shown, in the United States, many households and individuals have been affected by changes in family structure and gender roles, and the socioeconomic consequences have been substantial in terms of the level of inequality, children's life chances, and intergenerational transfers of advantage. The relatively severe consequences are in part due to the fact that the welfare state in the United States provides a relatively poor buffer against downward mobility in connection with divorce and against the risk of poverty in the case of single parenthood. A contributing factor is relatively strong selection into single parenthood of women (and some men) with low levels of education and poor family background. If most nonmarital childbearing was to well-educated women in their thirties, rather than to young poorly educated women, then the socioeconomic consequences would be considerably lower, and the effects on children smaller as well.

A recent cross-national study of the effect of children's school achievement in single- and two-parent families lends strong support to the notion that national differences may be quite pronounced (Pong et al. 2003). This study found that the effect of single parenthood on math and science achievement among third and fourth graders was strongest in the United States and New Zealand, and that "single parenthood is less detrimental when family policies equalize resources between single- and two-parent families" (Pong et al. 2003: 681). The study also found that the gap between children from single-parent and two-parent families were greater where single-parent families are more common.

Although the extent of change in family structure and gender roles and their socioeconomic consequences will be important mediating factors with regard to how much the stratification system has been affected by the Second Demographic Transition, it is important to keep in mind that even in societies where the socioeconomic consequences are relatively small—the Scandinavian countries come to mind—it is unlikely that social scientists therefore can conclude that changes in the composition of households, in children's family lives, and in women's economic roles will have no bearing on income inequality between households, children's achievements, or the openness of the intergenerational mobility regime. The effects will be smaller than what I here have described for the United States, but they will not be absent. This is partly because not all economic risks can be removed by even the most generous of welfare states, partly because there are other processes at work as well. The negative effects of growing up in a father-only family or in a stepfamily are testimony to that.

Notes

1. I thank Heike Trappe, Eva Bernhardt, and Ulla Björnberg for their constructive comments.

2. Eva Bernhardt pointed out to me that the questions I ask in this chapter are questions about the ways in which the stratification system may have been affected by key elements of the Second Demographic Transition.

3. Goldthorpe (1983) readily admitted that female-headed households should be included in mobility studies. This meant that it would be the occupational position of the head of the household, male or female, that would be used in measuring the family's class position.

4. I should note that I do not consider the role played by race and ethnicity to keep things relatively simple.

5. Households with incomes above $100,000 increased from a mere 3 percent in 1967 to 14 percent in 2002.

6. Measured by the employment status of the head of the household, and, if employed, by the occupational status measured by SEI.

7. Research in other countries have found similar results (Erikson and Jonsson 1993; Evans et al. 2003; Jonsson and Gähler 1997).

8. McLanahan and Sandefur (1994) compared the effect of living in a two-parent family with the effect of one year of mother's education and found them comparable. They estimated, for example, that if all children lived with both parents, the high school dropout rate would be lowered by 6 percent (McLanahan and Sandefur 1994: 43).

9. Breen and Goldthorpe (1997) use their model to explain why social class

differences in educational attainment has decreased in Sweden during the latter decades of the 20th century, pointing to the decrease in class differences in economic resources in Sweden during that period.

References

Acker, Joan. 1973. Women and Social Stratification: A Case of Intellectual Sexism. *American Journal of Sociology* 78:936–945.

Amato, Paul R. 2000. The Consequences of Divorce for Adults and Children. *Journal of Marriage and the Family* 62:1269–1287.

Amato, Paul. 2001. Children of Divorce in the 1990s: An Update of the Amato and Keith (1991) Meta-analysis. *Journal of Family Psychology* 15:355–370.

Biblarz, Timothy J. and Raftery, Adrian E. 1993. The Effects of Family Disruption on Social Mobility. *American Sociological Review* 58:97–109.

Biblarz, Timothy J., Raftery, Adrian E., and Bucur, Alexander. 1997. Family Structure and Social Mobility. *Social Forces* 75:1319–1341.

Biblarz, Timothy J. and Raftery, Adrian E. 1999. Family Structure, Educational Attainment, and Socioeconomic Success: Rethinking the "Pathology of Matriarchy." *American Journal of Sociology* 105:321–365.

Blau, Peter and Duncan, Otis D. 1967. *The American Occupational Structure*. New York: Wiley.

Breen, Richard and Goldthorpe, John. 1997. Explaining Social Class Differentials: Towards a Formal Rational Action Theory. *Rationality and Society* 9:275–287.

Cancian, Maria and Reed, Deborah. 1999. The Impact of Wives' Earnings on Income Inequality: Issues and Estimates. *Demography* 36:173–184.

Cherlin, Andrew J., Chase-Lansdale, P. L., and McRae, C. 1998. Effects of Parental Divorce on Mental Health throughout the Life Course. *American Sociological Review* 63:239–249.

Cherlin, Andrew J. Going to Extremes. 1999. Family Structure, Children's Wellbeing, and Social Science. *Demography* 36:421–428.

Crompton, Rosemary and Mann, Michael (eds.) 1986. *Gender and Stratification*. Cambridge: Polity.

Danziger, Sheldon. 1980. Do Working Wives Increase Family Income Inequality? *Journal of Human Resources* 15:444–451.

De Navas-Walt, Carmen, Cleveland, Robert, and Webster, Bruce H. Jr. 2003. *Income in the United States: 2002*. U.S. Census Bureau, Current Population Reports, P60-221. Washington D.C.: U.S. Government Printing Office.

DiPrete, Thomas. 2002. Life Course Risks, Mobility Regimes, and Mobility Consequences: A Comparison of Sweden, Germany, and the United States. *American Journal of Sociology* 108:267–309.

Erikson, Robert. 1984. Social Class of Men, Women and Families. *Sociology* 18:500–514

Erikson, Robert and Jonsson, Jan O. 1993. *Ursprung och Utbildung. Social snedre-krytering till högre studier.* Stockholm: SOU, 85

Erikson, Robert and Goldthorpe, John. 1992. *The Constant Flux.* Oxford: Oxford University Press.

Evans, Maria D. R., Kelley, Jonathan, and Wanner, R. A. 2003. Educational Attainment of Children of Divorce: Australia, 1940–90. *Journal of Sociology* 37: 275–297.

Featherman, David L. and Hauser, Robert M. 1978. *Opportunity and Change.* New York: Academic Press.

Gähler, Michael. 1998. Self-reported Psychological Well-being among Adult Children of Divorce in Sweden. *Acta Sociological* 41:209–225.

Goldthorpe, John H. 1983. Women and Class Analysis: In Defense of the Conventional View. *Sociology* 17:465–488.

Grusky David B. and DiPrete, Thomas. 1990. Recent Trends in the Process of Stratification. *Demography* 27:617–637.

Hanson, Thomas L. 1999. Does Parental Conflict Explain Why Divorce Is Negatively Associated with Child Welfare. *Social Forces* 77:1283–1316.

Hout, Michael. 1988. More Universalism, Less Structural Mobility: The American Occupational Structure in the 1980s. *American Journal of Sociology* 93: 1358–1400.

Jekielek, Susan M. 1998. Parental Conflict, Marital Disruption and Children's Emotional Well-being. *Social Forces* 76:905–935.

Jonsson Jan O. and Gähler, Michael. 1997. Family Dissolution, Family Reconstitution, and Children's Educational Careers: Recent Evidence for Sweden. *Demography* 34:277–293.

Kalmijn, Matthijs. 1994. Mother's Occupational Status and Children's Schooling. *American Sociological Review* 59:257–275.

Karoly, Lynn A. and Burtless, Gary. 1995. Demographic Change, Rising Earnings Inequality, and the Distribution of Personal Well-being, 1959–1989. *Demography* 32:379n405.

Lesthaeghe, Ron. 1995. The Second Demographic Transition. An Interpretation. Pp. 17–62. In Karen O. Mason and An-Magrit Jensen (eds.) *Gender and Family Change in Industrialized Countries.* Oxford: Clarendon

Levy, Frank. 1997. *The New Dollars and Dreams: American Incomes and Economic Change.* New York: Russell Sage Foundation.

Mare, Robert D. 1995. Changes in Educational Attainment and School Enrollment. Pp. 155–214. In Reynolds Farley (ed.) *State of the Union. America in the 1990s.* New York: Russell Sage Foundation.

Mayer, Susan E. 2001. How Did the Increase in Economic Inequality between 1970 and 1990 Affect Children's Educational Attainment? *American Journal of Sociology* 107:1–32.

McLanahan Sara S. and Sandefur, Gary. 1994. *Growing Up with a Single Parent.* Cambridge: Harvard University Press.

Moore, Kristin Anderson and Redd, Zakia. 2002. *Children in Poverty: Trends, Consequences, and Policy Options*. Child Trends. Research Brief #2002-54. Washington D.C.

NiBhrolcháin, Máire. 2001. "Divorce Effects" and Causality in the Social Sciences. *European Sociological Review* 17:33–58.

Pong, Suet-Ling, Dronkers, Joop, and Hampden-Thompson, Gillian. 2003. Family Policies and Children's School Achievement in Single- versus Two-parent Families. *Journal of Marriage and the Family* 65:681–699.

Popenoe, David. 1996. *Disturbing the Nest. Family Change and Decline in Modern Societies*. New York: Aldine de Gruyter.

Rainwater, Lee and Smeeding, Timothy M. 2003. *Poor Kids in a Rich Country: America's Children in Comparative Perspective*. New York: Russell Sage Foundation.

Ryscavage, Paul, Green, Gordon, and Welnak, Edward. 1992. The Impact of Demographic, Social and Economic Change on the Distribution of Income. In Studies in the Distribution of Income. *Current Population Reports*, ser. P-60, no. 183. Washington, DC: U.S. Government Printing Office.

Sørensen, Annemette. 1994. Women, Family and Class. *Annual Review of Sociology* 20:27–47.

Sørensen, Annemette. 2004. Economic Relations Between Women and Men: New Realities and the Re-Interpretation of Dependence. Pp. 281–98. In Janet Z. Giele and Elke Holst (eds.) *Changing Life Patterns in Western Industrial Societies*. Advances in Life Course Research, Vol. 8. Oxford: Elsevier.

Szelényi, Szonja. 2001. The "Woman Problem" in Stratification Theory and Research. Pp. 681–88. In David B. Grusky (ed.) *Social Stratification. Class, Race, and Gender in Sociological Perspective*. 2nd Ed. Boulder, Colo.: Westview.

CHAPTER SIX

Inequalities in Later Life: Gender, Marital Status, and Health Behaviors

Sara Arber

Theorists of social stratification have paid scant attention to inequalities in later life. This is surprising given that the period of the life course after the cessation of paid work is becoming almost as long as the average period of life spent in paid employment. Lives are lengthening, the expectation of life in England in 2000 was 80 years for women and 76 years for men (ONS 2003), yet the average age at which men and women exit the labor market has decreased markedly over the last twenty years. In their early sixties, only a minority of men and barely 10 percent of women are in paid employment. Despite these major societal changes, writers on social stratification have neglected the structured nature of inequalities in the postretirement phase of the life course, which may last a quarter of a century or longer.

Aging theorists have contrasted later life with earlier periods of the life course, and put forward alternative theoretical frameworks for understanding inequality in later life. These frameworks include the *leveling hypothesis* that argues that class (racial and other) differences over the life course are leveled (or homogenized) in old age as groups become more alike, regardless of their starting point. *Structural dependency theories* have also emphasized societal mechanisms that result in the poverty and material disadvantage of older people as a group (Phillipson 1982). In contrast, *continuity theory* emphasizes that the nature, extent, and drivers of inequality in later life remain constant from working life through to the postretirement phase. A more recent approach suggests that later life is a time of *cumulative advantage/disadvantage* resulting in increased inequality in later life. It is argued that economic advantages from earlier in the life course lead to greater accumulation of further advantages, and similarly disadvantages are compounded in later life (O'Rand 1996).

The applicability of each of these theories as explanations for the nature of inequalities among older people vis-à-vis working age cohorts varies between societies and across historical time within the same society. For example, in the UK, the leveling hypothesis was more applicable in the 1950s and 1960s when older people in the UK were disproportionately poor and a more homogenous group. Whereas, the extensive growth of private pensions in the 1980s and 1990s has resulted in profound inequality among older people, and thus theoretical arguments of *continuity* and *accumulated advantage/disadvantage* have come to the fore.

Although the above theoretical approaches draw contrasts between the older and the working age population, the concern in this chapter is to explore the structural basis of diversity among older people. In the United States, older black people have been seen as facing a *double jeopardy* associated with both their minority status and old age (Pampel 1998). Such approaches have added in older women, and discussed this factor in terms of *triple jeopardy* to highlight the multiple disadvantages that certain groups of individuals face in old age (Norman 1985; Calasanti and Slevin 2001). However, this additive approach implicitly assumes that all members of certain groups are privileged (such as midlife, white men) while others are disadvantaged (such as older, black women). Arber and Ginn (1991) address gender inequalities in later life from a *political economy* perspective, advocating the need to analyze a wide range of inequalities resulting from the power relations that structure society.

McMullin (1995) has examined why gender relations and age relations have been neglected in sociological theory, and criticized "add on" theoretical approaches, for example that add on gender to sociological theories of aging (or add on age relations to feminist theory). She emphasizes the need to rethink the interconnections between gender, age, and class: "Social class has to be reconceptualized by thinking about age and gendered processes that influence the relations of distribution and production" (p. 41). A key aspect of these gendered processes relates to marital relations across the life course, and this chapter argues that these processes take on particular salience in structuring inequality in later life.

The life course has become a dominant organizing concept in studies of later life, with writers emphasizing both the influence of various transitions across the life course and the continuity of aspects of earlier lives through into later life (Bury 1995; Arber and Evandrou 1993). Life course approaches have built on earlier work of family sociologists who highlighted the differential biographies of women and men (Hareven and Adams 1982), and thus how later life is gendered as a consequence of the differentiated nature of women's and men's lives. Key issues relate to experiences of marriage and childbearing, and how these impact on economic roles, ability to accumulate pensions, and patterns of social connectivity. However, the work of family sociologists on gendered lives has tended to neglect the ways in which older men's lives have also been gendered by their marital biography. Thus, the nature of continuity from adult to later life or accumulation of advantage/disadvantage may differ for men and women associated with their marital history.

The chapter focuses on the marital status of older women and men as a way of capturing aspects of gendered biographies as they impact on the lived experience of later life. The interconnections with class, material well-being, and social connectivity will be explored to assess evidence of particular disadvantage or advantage among older women and men with specific marital histories. The argument is extended to examine whether identified material and social disadvantages matter for other aspects of well-being in later life. There has been extensive research on inequalities in health, although less has focused on later life, and very little research has addressed inequalities in health behaviors in later life. The chapter therefore uses health behaviors as an exemplar to explore the extent to which the marital positionings of women and men in later life impact on their smoking and alcohol consumption, even after taking into account inequalities in class, material circumstances, and social connectivity. The aim throughout is to assess how gender and marital status interact in later life to lead to more or less advantaged life chances.

Women form the majority in later life, with the numerical gender differential becoming more unbalanced as age advances. For example, in the UK in 2001, there were 138 women aged 65+ for every 100 men, and 259 women for every 100 men aged 85 and over (Arber and Ginn 2004). Therefore, any social structural analysis of inequalities in later life has to take seriously the measurement of class and other indicators of inequality for older women (because they form the majority).

CLASS IN LATER LIFE

With expansion of higher education and earlier labor market exit, the dominance of the paid working career may have become shorter in a temporal sense, but is becoming more important in structuring the experiences of life outside these core working ages. For an older person, class based on their last main occupation remains an important differentiator of their life chances—their pension income, likely accumulation of cultural capital, and their health. The life course acquisition of pension entitlements has become a critical determinant in the UK of financial resources and quality of life in retirement (Ginn 2003). While acknowledging the privileged position of class as a determinant of material well-being in later life, there are important issues that have been relatively neglected in terms of how class intersects with gender in later life.

At earlier stages of the life course, married women have traditionally been analyzed in terms of their husband's class position, which Goldthorpe (1983) characterized as "the conventional approach." I (1997) examined the value of this approach, compared with an "individualistic" approach, for those of working age. In later life, the "conventional approach" is untenable because only a minority of women over age 65 have a husband on whom their class position could potentially be based. Men's higher level of mortality, together with the gendered cultural convention of men being older than their marital partner, means that widowhood is normative for women in later life. Therefore, older women's own previous occupation is proposed as an indicator of their class position (Arber and Ginn 1993). However, among the current generation of older women, measuring class using their own last main occupation may potentially be considered problematic because many women from this generation worked only part time or intermittently following marriage. Thus, class measured in this way may be a less powerful indicator of resources in later life for older women than for older men. This is an empirical question that deserves greater attention by students of stratification.

The potential concerns about using last main occupation as an indicator of class in later life, particularly for older women, leads to the supposition that greater attention should be paid to current financial or material circumstances as structural indicators of inequality. The chapter therefore examines how gender and marital status are associated with both class (based on main occupation in the paid workforce during working life) and current financial or material circumstances among older men and women.

MARITAL STATUS AND GENDER IN LATER LIFE

Family sociologists have emphasized interlinked lives and family transitions across the life course and how these are associated with caring and social connectedness. One of the key transitions in later life is widowhood; therefore, any analysis of social stratification in later life must address widowhood and how this differs by gender. In addition, the contours of later life are changing as a higher proportion of cohorts enter later life as divorced, yet there is little recognition of the structured inequalities associated with the lives of older divorced women and men (Arber et al. 2003).

Marital status is a pivotal differentiating feature in later life. This chapter addresses whether this is more so for women than men. For older women in England and Wales, widowhood is normative, almost half of all women over 65 are widowed, and the proportions rapidly rise with age (see Table 6.1). The norm for older men is to be married, with the majority of older men still married when they die. Seventy percent of men over age 65 in England and Wales are married. For men below 80, the proportions married fall only slowly with advancing age. Even in their early eighties, 61 percent of men are married, falling to half in their late eighties, and still a third in their nineties. This contrasts markedly with older women, where the proportion married falls from 56 percent in their late sixties to under a quarter by their early eighties. It is very unusual for a woman in her nineties to still be married, under 6 percent. However, the dominance of marriage for men should not blind researchers to a consideration of the minority experience of widowhood, facing 17 percent of men over 65. Twenty-nine percent of men in their early eighties are widowed, which rapidly climbs to over 40 percent in their late eighties.

Among current cohorts of older people, relatively small proportions are divorced or separated, only 6 percent of men and women over 65 (see Table 6.1). However, this figure varies with age, from 9 percent in their late sixties to only 2 percent above age 85. These age differences reflect the growth over the last thirty years in divorce at younger ages. Projections for the UK suggest that by 2021, the proportion of older men and women who are divorced will more than double to 13 percent of men and 14 percent of

TABLE 6.1

Marital Status by Gender and Age,
England and Wales, 2001, Age 65+
(Row Percentages)

Age Group	Married	Widowed	Divorced/ Separated	Never Married	Total	% Aged 65+ (millions)
(a) Men						
65–69	76.5	6.9	9.2	7.5	100%	31.5
70–74	73.7	11.9	6.7	7.7	100%	27.0
75–79	68.3	20.2	4.6	7.0	100%	21.0
80–84	60.9	29.1	3.3	6.7	100%	12.4
85–89	49.1	42.8	2.4	5.6	100%	5.9
90+	33.3	56.4	2.1	8.1	100%	2.2
						100%
Total 65+	69.6	17.0	6.2	7.2	100%	3.49
(b) Women						
65–69	55.7	21.4	9.1	4.8	100%	24.7
70–74	49.9	37.1	7.0	6.0	100%	23.5
75–79	36.8	52.0	4.8	6.5	100%	21.2
80–84	23.8	65.5	3.5	7.2	100%	15.4
85–89	12.1	77.3	2.3	8.2	100%	9.8
90+	5.7	81.5	1.7	11.0	100%	5.4
						100%
Total 65+	39.8	47.6	6.0	6.6	100%	4.82

SOURCE: ONS, 2003. *Census 2001. National Report for England and Wales*, London: The Stationary Office, derived from Table S002.

women over 65 (Shaw 1999). These are rapid demographic changes, projecting as many older divorced men as widowers by 2021. Therefore, over the coming years it will be increasingly important to consider to what extent divorced older men and women face particularly disadvantaged life chances.

The marital status of older people reflects their prior life course as well as their current situation. For both men and women, being married in later life represents substantial continuities in gender roles and relationships even in their eighties. For older men, their wife usually continues to provide domestic services, support, and care, except in the minority of cases where a wife is frail or disabled and husbands take over caring roles (Davidson et al. 2000). The normativity of heterosexual masculinity remains for the majority of these older married men. Widowhood for men means loss of the support and caring received from a wife, and thus of the gendered power relationship a man may have held for most of his life as a "breadwinner" and vis-à-vis his wife.

Widows and widowers have had and lost a marital partner. The death of a companion, confidante, and major source of emotional and practical support can represent a profound loss to older men and women (Askham 1994; Davidson 1999), but their current family ties, social networks, and material situation in turn reflects their gender and that they were married, often for most of their lives. Divorcees on the other hand may have disrupted family relationships. Older divorced men particularly are likely to have weak contacts with children and grandchildren and report less practical and emotional support from family and friends than married men (Solomou et al. 1998). The divorced may have suffered significant financial hardship during their working lives associated with marital breakdown, particularly as many divorced women become lone mothers, and many divorced men experience unemployment (Price and Ginn 2003).

Older people who remained single throughout their life may have particular characteristics that led them not to marry, are unlikely to have had children, and their work patterns and social interactions may reflect both these things. Never married women from these generations are more likely than married women to have been "career" women, with formal marriage bars operating on UK civil servants and teachers until the mid-1940s, while there were strong social norms operating against married women working in the years immediately after World War II.

Late life research has paid more attention to marital status differentials among women than men (Ginn and Arber 1999; Ginn et al. 2001). For example, there has been scant UK work on the material circumstances of older men who are divorced, never married, or widowed (Price and Ginn, 2003). This situation contrasts with older women, where extensive cross-national research has demonstrated the adverse consequences of widowhood and divorce for older women's income and pensions (Ginn et al. 2001). The implicit assumption has been that the financial position of older men is unaffected by partnership breakdown, whether through widowhood or divorce, with a corresponding lack of attention to the financial and material circum-

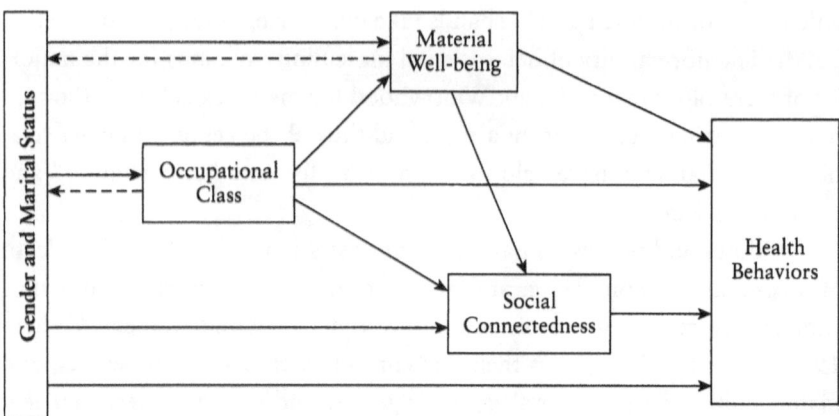

Figure 6.1.   Conceptual Model of Inequalities in Health Behavior in Later Life

stances of divorced or widowed older men. In later life, material wealth and pension accumulation, and patterns of family contact and friendship all reflect the life lived to date. The present material circumstances and social relationships of older people can only be understood by reference to their past, both present and past being reflected in the categorization of marital status.

AIMS

This chapter examines how the intersection of gender and marital status in later life in Britain is associated with three areas of advantage/disadvantage, namely class based on main occupation during working life, current material resources, and access to social support from family, friends, and neighbors. A model of the ways in which these three areas of advantage/disadvantage may be linked to gender and marital status is shown in Figure 6.1. The chapter also focuses on inequalities in two adverse health behaviors: smoking and drinking alcohol above the recommended level, examining to what extent class, differential material resources, and social support from family and friends can explain differences in these two health behaviors according to gender and marital status groups.[1]

The initial sections of the chapter examine (1) how marital status in later life is associated with class, based on main occupation during working life, but in gender differentiated ways associated with the older person's life course; (2) how the interaction of gender and marital status is associated with current material resources in later life; and (3) how the marital status of older men and women is linked to disadvantage in terms of social connectedness to family, friends, and neighbors. The chapter then turns to an examination of inequalities in health behaviors according to gender and marital status, analyzing to what extent differences in smoking and alcohol consumption according to marital status and gender can be explained by inequalities in class, current material resources, and level of social connectedness.

DATA AND METHODS

To adequately address the model in Figure 6.1 would require longitudinal data. However, there are no British longitudinal datasets on the aging population that are large enough to yield sufficient numbers of older people who are divorced and never married, and thus allow a full analysis of how the intersection of gender and marital status is linked to structural factors, and to health behavior. Therefore, a number of years of a large annual cross-sectional survey are combined for analysis.

The British General Household Survey (GHS) is a nationally representative survey of about 10,000 households per year, in which all persons age 16 and over are interviewed, with a response rate of around 80 percent in the mid-1990s (Walker at al. 2001). For the analysis of class and material circumstances, five years of data are combined—1993–96 and 1998 (there was no GHS conducted in 1997), yielding a sample of about 17,000 men and women aged 65 and over. The GHS asked questions on smoking and alcohol consumption in alternate years, 1994, 1996, and 1998. Questions about contacts with family and friends are asked periodically, and for these analyses, the 1994 and 1998 GHS data were combined. The datasets are sufficiently large to provide reliable estimates for small subgroups, such as never married older women and divorced older men. Only 1 percent of people over age 65 were cohabiting and they are combined with the married; similarly, the separated and divorced have been combined.

The GHS is a sample of people living in the community, and therefore omits people living in residential or nursing homes. The likelihood of entering a care home increases with advancing age, reaching 23 percent of women and 12 percent of men over age 85 at the 2001 census, with residence in a care home strongly differentiated by marital status and gender (Arber and Ginn 2004). The never married were most likely to live in a care home, and the married were least likely. The widowed fall between these two extremes. Thus, when analyzing older people according to marital status using the GHS, it is important to recognize that those living in the community are a selected group, and that the health selection criteria for entry into a care home differ by marital status, especially at advanced ages.

CLASS AND MARITAL STATUS IN LATER LIFE

Class has historically been a key dimension within analyses of stratification, but little attention has been paid to how the link between marital status and class in later life is gender differentiated. Because few older people are in paid employment, this section uses a life course measure of class for both older men and women, namely their last main occupation during working life. Marital status in later life partly reflects much earlier life course "decisions" about whether to partner and partnership breakdown. The majority of older people have been married, and as discussed earlier the majority of men, but not women, remain married until their eighties.

How class intersects with marital status in later life reflects gender roles and the play over the life course of earlier patterns of advantage and disadvantage. Married men in later life are the most advantaged group in terms of class, with the highest proportion previously in professional and managerial occupations (classes I and II), and few in semiskilled and unskilled occupations (classes IV and V), see Table 6.2. Their occupational class contrasts with married older women, who are less likely than other women to have been in professional and managerial occupations. These findings illustrate the ways in which the breadwinner ideology for this generation of older married men resulted in greater occupational achievement, but constrained the occupational achievement of their wives, relative to that of their never married sisters.

Never married men and women in later life differ fundamentally by class. Older women who never married were often "career" women and chose not to marry because of perceived constraints of marriage on their career, often becoming teachers, nurses, and other professionals. Table 6.2b shows that among older women, those who never married are most likely to have been in a professional or managerial class and least likely to have undertaken lower working class jobs (classes IV and V).

Given that marriage was normative for the older generation, some men

TABLE 6.2
Class[1] by Marital Status for Men and Women
Age 65–74 and Age 75+
(Column Percentages)

	Married	Widowed	Divorced/ Separated	Never Married	Total
(a) Men					
65–74					
Class I+II	35	20	20	26	32
Class IIInm	10	12	11	11	11
Class IIIm	36	42	41	29	36
Class IV+V	19	26	28	34	21
Total 65–74	100%	100%	100%	100%	100%
N=	3,663	527	234	292	4,716
75+					
Class I+II	36	29	19	22	33
Class IIInm	13	10	17	12	12
Class IIIm	33	37	36	34	34
Class IV+V	18	24	28	31	21
Total 75+	100%	100%	100%	100%	100%
N=	1,733	826	69	134	2,762
(b) Women					
65–74					
Class I+II	18	17	23	31	19
Class IIInm	38	32	33	38	36
Class IIIm	11	12	14	10	11
Class IV+V	33	40	30	21	34
Total 65–74	100%	100%	100%	100%	100%
N=	2,944	1,873	277	323	5,417
75+					
Class I+II	15	17	24	31	18
Class IIInm	37	30	26	34	32
Class IIIm	12	13	15	15	13
Class IV+V	36	39	35	19	37
Total 75+	100%	100%	100%	100%	100%
N=	1,057	2,626	138	343	4,164

[1] Class is based on the individual's last main occupation during working life, coded according to the Registrar General's social classes.

SOURCE: General Household Survey, 1993, 1994, 1995, 1996, and 1998 (author's analysis)

who did not marry may have been unsuccessful in the "marriage market" due to their weaker class position, being in a job without prospects, or being in an occupational institutional culture such as the military. Men who did not marry were by definition not "breadwinners," therefore may have felt less pressure to perform occupationally or materially in terms of being a "good provider," and thus not have achieved as much as equivalent married men in terms of class, income, or pension accumulation. Table 6.2a shows that never married men are the group of men most likely to be in lower working class occupations (classes IV and V). However, a slightly higher percentage of never married than divorced men were in class I and II jobs, suggesting that it is too simple to consider never married older men solely as failures in the marriage market because of their lack of occupational potential.

Divorced older men are the least likely to be in a higher occupational class. Being divorced in later life for men is linked to three types of selection factors. First, class and material position may be implicated in the likelihood of divorce, as those of a lower class and poorer material circumstances are somewhat more likely to divorce. Second, repartnering and remarriage among divorced men is higher than for divorced women and is more likely among divorced men with greater financial and other types of resources. Thus, the pool of divorced men in later life will be disproportionately composed of those with less material resources, and also poor health may reduce remarriage rates. These selection effects may be less evident for women, where factors such as whether the woman has children have a greater effect on their probability of remarriage, although poor health may also affect whether divorced women remarry. Only longitudinal data can tease out the differential patterns of selection into and out of divorce for men and women and how they interconnect with class, material resources, and health.

Third, there may be a direct effect of divorce on occupational class that is differential for women and men. For women, divorce often stimulates return to the labor market (or higher education); thus, some divorced women regain or develop careers, entering middle class or professional occupations later in life. Table 6.2b shows that divorced older women have the second highest proportion in class I and II occupations, following never married women, and similarly are the second least likely marital status group to be in lower class occupations. However, divorce for men may have the opposite labor force participation effect, often compounded by requirements to make child maintenance payments. Without the need to fulfil the breadwinner ideology, and often an antipathy to paying money to an estranged wife, may decrease the incentives of divorced men to be financially successful.

The extensive class inequalities in health literature (Bartley et al. 1998; Mackenbach and Bakker 2002) suggest a strong causal pathway between occupational class and being a widow/widower, given that countless UK studies show a linear relationship between class and mortality. It is therefore expected that those who are widowed, especially at younger ages, will be more likely to be working class. However, with increasing age, the class selection into widowhood is likely to diminish, and probably disappears almost entirely among widows and widowers in their eighties. Table 6.2b shows that among women, widows are the group most likely to have been in lower working class occupations, supporting a class and health selection argument. Because women are much more likely to be widowed than men, researchers would expect the class selection mechanisms associated with widowhood to be greater for widows than widowers, which is indeed the case from Table 6.2. Thus, among men, widowers stand intermediate between the married and divorced in class terms, with their class disadvantage somewhat greater among younger widowers (age 65–74) than older widowers over age 75 (as would be expected from selection on class-related mortality grounds).

This section has begun to address the complex causal pathways between older men's and women's marital status and their class (based on last main occupation). Although the cross-sectional data used in this chapter cannot address directions of causality, it can highlight the extent to which any research on the marital status of older people means discussing groups that differ substantially in terms of their class position, but in gender-differentiated ways.

MATERIAL INEQUALITY AND MARITAL STATUS IN LATER LIFE

Research on material inequalities among older people has paid relatively little attention to marital status and gender, except with regard to pensions among older women (Ginn 2003). Three aspects of material inequality are examined in this section: having a low household income, lacking a household car, and renting (rather than owning) a home. Table 6.3a presents logistic regression analyses, for each of these indicators of material disadvantage. In each case, married men are defined as the reference category with

TABLE 6.3

Odds Ratios[d] of (a) Material Circumstances and (b) Social Connectedness by Gender and Marital Status in Britain, Age 65+

	MEN				WOMEN			
	Married	Widowed	Divorced/ Separated	Never Married	Married	Widowed	Divorced/ Separated	Never Married
(a) *Material Circumstances*								
(i) Household Income[a,b] in Lowest 25% of Those 65+	1.0	1.3**	2.2**	1.5*	1.2*	2.7**	4.7**	1.8**
(ii) Does Not Own Home – i.e. Renter	1.0	1.9**	4.5**	3.0**	1.1	2.1**	3.6**	2.0**
(iii) No Car in Household	1.0	2.0**	3.5**	4.2**	1.2**	7.5**	7.0**	5.4**
(b) *Social contact*[c]								
(i) Rarely *Hosts* Friends/Family	1.0	1.9**	4.3**	5.4**	1.0	0.9	1.5	2.5**
(ii) Rarely *Visits* Friends/Family	1.0	0.9	1.8**	2.3**	1.0	1.1	0.9	1.0
(iii) Rarely *Chats* with Neighbors	1.0	1.1	3.1**	1.8**	1.3*	1.6**	1.7*	1.7**
Min N = (a)	4,673	1,196	284	389	3,651	4,160	372	596
Min N = (b)	1,966	516	118	162	1,564	1,787	162	248

NB. Odds ratios above 4.0 are highlighted in dark gray and above 2.0 are highlighted in pale gray

[a] Household income and personal income adjusted according to Retail Price Index 1998

[b] Household income was equalized for household composition using the McClements scale

[c] Social contacts are based on those who rarely or less than once a month (i) *host* friends or family in their own home, (ii) *visit* friends or family members, and (iii) *chat* to neighbors

[d] Odds ratios after controlling for 5 year age groups (65–9, 70–4, 75–9, 80–4, 85+); reference category is married men with odds defined as 1.0

Significance of difference from the reference category, married men, *p < 0.05, **p < 0.01

SOURCE: *General Household Survey*, (a) Material circumstances—1993–96, 1998; (b) Social contact—1994 and 1998.

odds of 1.00. The interaction of gender and marital status is examined; any gender/marital status category with an odds ratio higher than 1.00 has a greater likelihood of being materially disadvantaged than married men.

Household income is measured as those falling into the lowest quartile (25 percent) of the income distribution of those over age 65. Income levels have been adjusted to 1998 values using the Retail Price Index, and the older person's household composition has been adjusted using the McClements income equivalizing scales (Department of Work and Pensions 2002). Equivalized household income allows the direct comparison of living standards of older people according to marital status. Income in later life is largely linked to accumulation of pensions during working life, and whether pensions are inherited on the death of a spouse. Inequality between rich and poor pensioners, linked to class and gender, has grown over the last thirty years, as the UK pension system has been increasingly privatized (Ginn and Arber 1999; Ginn 2003).

Divorced women are the group most likely to be poor in later life with an odds ratio of household poverty of 4.7 compared with married men (OR = 1.0), followed by widows (OR = 2.7); see Table 6.3a. The latter financial disadvantage is particularly salient, as almost half of older women are widows. The household income of widowers is not very different from that of married men, showing that among men there is little financial penalty attached to widowhood. Divorced men stand out as the most financially disadvantaged group of older men (OR = 2.2). Among women living without a partner, never married women are less likely to live in a household in poverty. Most never married women have been in the labor market throughout their working life and are the group of older women most likely to have accumulated their own occupational pension. Although there are household income differences between groups of older men, with divorced men being the most disadvantaged, there are much larger income differences among older women by marital status.

Home ownership is an indicator of material inequality. In the UK, housing tenure has increasingly come to represent a social divide, with rented accommodation disproportionately found in socially and economically deprived neighborhoods. These neighborhoods are also more likely to have problems of safety and security, adversely affecting social relations with friends and neighbors. Home ownership represents an asset from which older people can potentially release capital and is associated generally with greater capital wealth.

Married men and women are the most advantaged in home ownership, with divorced men and women the most disadvantaged (Table 6.3a). Divorced older men have an odds ratio of 4.5 of renting their home, which is even higher than for divorced women (OR = 3.6). The latter reflects divorced women's very disadvantaged financial circumstances in later life. Divorced older men's high level of renting is probably because of both their lower financial resources and divorce settlements where an owned marital home was transferred to their wife in order to house dependent children of the marriage, leaving men renting accommodation. Never married men have much higher odds of renting in later life (OR = 3.0) than married men, whereas the housing situation of never married women (OR = 2.0) is better than that of never married men.

There is little difference in the housing position of widows and widowers; both have an odds ratio of living in rented accommodation of around 2.0 compared to their married counterparts (OR = 1.0). This finding suggests that during widowhood, some older people move into rented accommodation, because they cannot afford the upkeep of an owned home, to move nearer other family members, or to move into sheltered accommodation. Renting is associated with widowhood per se, because there are no clear differences by gender.

Car ownership indicates both that a household has sufficient material resources to own, run, and maintain a car, and facilitates independence—the ability to shop, visit, enjoy leisure facilities, help with grandchildren, attend hospital appointments, and so forth. Among the current cohort of older people, car ownership varies fundamentally by gender; all groups of women without a partner are disadvantaged in their access to a car in the household compared with married women or men. This reflects the absence of driving skills, or the cessation of driving by older women due to failing health, and the very disadvantaged financial position of previously married women. The greatest differential is for widows, with odds of not having a car 7.5 times greater than the odds for married men. The odds ratio for divorced women is 7.0 and for never married women is 5.4. Thus, for women, widowhood or divorce may represent more than the loss of a breadwinner and partner—having a profound impact by restricting their mobility through removing access to a car in the household. Never married women are less disadvantaged, probably because they were more likely to learn to drive when younger, as well as being relatively better off and so have the resources to afford to run a car in later life.

There is a strong gradient in car ownership among men by marital status. Married men are the most likely to have a car, followed by widowers (OR = 2.0), divorced men (OR = 3.5), and never married men are least likely to have a car (OR = 4.2). The lower level of car ownership for divorced and never married older men may partly reflect their low household income.

On all three measures of material household well-being, older married people are highly advantaged. This gender similarity of the advantage of married older men and women must be tempered by the recognition that 70 percent of older men, but only 40 percent of older women, are married (Table 6.1). Widows, constituting about half of all older women, have twice the odds of both living in poverty and of renting their home compared with their married counterparts. There are less striking differences in the material well-being of the smaller group of widowed men compared to the majority group of married older men. Thus, gender effects the structural impact of marital status, with widowhood having a major adverse effect on the material well-being of older women, but less so for older men.

The proportionately small groups of divorced women and men are very disadvantaged on all three measures of material well-being. They are the most likely to rent their home and have a low household income. There may have been a direct effect of divorce on material resources, which is differentiated for women and men. Although women following divorce often return to the labor market, it is usually very difficult for them to recoup an adequate pension position following late reentry.

For women to have been partnered, and lost their husband through death or divorce, has profound implications for their material well-being in later life. But this adverse effect is usually more severe for divorced women, for whom there is no possibility of inheriting a proportion of a husband's pension, and for whom there may have been material privations earlier in life because of divorce, which have then followed the woman through her life course, becoming compounded with time. In contrast, there are fewer material effects of widowhood for men, as most men's pension position is only marginally affected in "real terms" following the death of their wife.

The meaning of being never married differs markedly by gender in later life, reflecting gendered relations across the life course. The gendered routes to remaining lifelong single among this cohort of older people are quite dissimilar, and the consequences of these divergent routes lead to gender differences in material well-being. Never married women are in an advantaged material situation in later life relative to other women without a partner: they are less likely to have a low income, more likely to have a car, and more likely to own their home. These differences reflect their greater attachment to the labor market, compared with ever-married women whose employment careers were constrained by caring. In contrast, never married men are the least likely to own a car and are much less likely to own their home than widowers.

This section has shown the importance of analyzing the intersection between gender and marital status when analyzing material well-being in later life. Being married is beneficial for older men and women in terms of material well-being, while both divorced women and men are structurally disadvantaged. The never married show a divergent pattern by gender, with never married women relatively advantaged compared to other nonpartnered older women, whereas never married men show a broadly comparable level of disadvantage to divorced men. The position of the widowed diverges according to gender, with widowers relatively more similar to married men, but a larger material gap between widows and married women. These findings suggest the importance of gender relations as a life course process in explaining the differential impact of marital status on material well-being in later life.

SOCIAL RELATIONSHIPS AND MARITAL STATUS

Marital status in later life is associated with broader social relationships, such as contacts with both family and friends. There is likely to be substantial continuity of patterns of relationships with family and friends from the adult years through to later life. The gendered organization of caring for both children and partners means that older married, widowed, and divorced women's employment careers are likely to have been constrained by caring responsibilities. However, at the same time, the gendered nature of caregiving across the life course will have increased the social connectedness of women, enriching women's social networks in later life. Women are traditionally the "kin keepers," therefore married men who become widowed or divorced may not only lose their wife, but also their social connection with wider family members and mutual friends.

Social contact with family members and with friends is critical for health and well-being (Cohen 1988, Umbersen 1992), providing buffers and emotional support in times of stress (Cooper et al. 1999b). De Jong Gierveld (2003) shows how older people living alone are less likely to report loneliness where they have more contact with both family and friends, and Farquhar (1995) and Bowling (1995) have both identified relationships with family and friends as of key importance to the quality of life of older people.

The ability to form and maintain social relationships is in many ways linked to gender and marital status, as well as material resources. Older women tend to have more extensive networks of friends than older men, and older women more often develop new friendships in later life than older men (Allan 1985; Jerrome 1996). Marriage provides an important social supportive relationship in later life and marital status differentiates informal social support, especially among men (Wenger et al. 1996). When individuals are asked about the person to whom they feel most emotionally "close" or can confide in, the marital partner is more often nominated as the "closest" person by married men than by married women (Fuhrer et al. 1999). The marital relationship seems to be particularly important for older men (Askham 1994; Davidson 1999). Married men often do not form emotionally close supportive relationships with friends, and their wives provide a key supportive role in this respect (Finch and Mason 1993).

Older widowers may be disadvantaged by a weakening of family contacts, and a lack of social support because of both their smaller network of friends, and their more distant relationships with children and other family members than is the case for older widows (Davidson 2000). Solomou et al. (1998) found that divorced and never married older men reported less practical and emotional support from family and friends than married men. Divorced older men in the Netherlands have less contact with family members than widowed men or divorced older women, largely because of attenuated relationships with their children (de Jong Gierveld 2003). Widowed older people may seek to replace their lost partner by greater involvement with family members and wider kin and with friends as a compensation, and as an alternative source of companionship and identity.

Social connectedness may take the form of family relations, friendships, and contact with neighbors, each of which contributes in a different way to quality of life (Phillipson et al. 2001). With advancing age, social interactions increasingly take place in the private sphere of the older person's own home, in the home of relatives or friends, or with neighbors. Neighbors can be an important source of social contact for older people, who spend more time in their local area than those of working age. Neighborhood interaction may vary from fairly brief standardized greetings to more lengthy interactions and possibly exchange of favors between neighbors (Perren et al. 2004). Chatting with neighbors, therefore, provides another indicator of the degree of social connectedness of older people.

This section examines how the intersection of gender and marital status is associated with three measures of social connectedness linked to interactions in the private sphere of the home, namely those who say they *host* family or friends, *visit* family or friends, or *chat to neighbors* less than monthly or never, which is characterized as "rarely." That is, older people who are relatively isolated from social interactions in their own home and in the homes of relatives or friends, and rarely interact with neighbors. (Analyses of older people's social contacts in public settings, such as different types of social organizations, are reported in Arber [2004] and Perren et al. [2003]).

The three measures of social contact are analyzed using logistic regression models as in the previous section. There is much greater variation in the extensiveness of social connectedness among men according to marital status than among women (see Table 6.3b). These findings differ markedly from those for material well-being.

Table 6.3b suggests that older men living without a partner are much less likely to *host* others in their home than married men, indicating that wives are the major instigators of such home-based social interactions. However, there is little difference in *visiting* between married and widowed men, suggesting that widowers are invited to the home of family members and friends to the same extent as married men. Never married men are the least likely to visit relatives and friends, followed by divorced men. In relation to chatting with neighbors, there is a significant difference among men, with a division between married men and widowers on the one hand, and divorced and never married men on the other. Divorced men are least likely to speak to neighbors (OR = 3.1), followed by never married men (OR = 1.8). The findings suggest that these two groups of older men are relatively isolated from relatives, friends, and neighbors, which may lead to loneliness and lack of access to potential sources of social and instrumental support.

There is no association between an older woman's marital status and her likelihood of *visiting* relatives or friends or chatting to neighbors. However, the likelihood of *hosting* relatives and friends is significantly lower for never married women (OR = 2.5) than either married women or widows.

This section has shown that divorced and never married men are the groups least likely to be involved in social contacts with relatives and friends in the home environment, and with neighbors, and are therefore vulnerable to social isolation. This lack of social connectedness means that they may both lack "watchful" significant others who may moderate damaging health behaviors, and also they are more likely to lack social supports that act as buffers to social stress, potentially leading to higher levels of health damaging behaviors, such as smoking and drinking.

HEALTH BEHAVIORS IN LATER LIFE

Extensive research on marital status and health shows that married men have better health than never married or previously married men (Morgan 1980; Wyke and Ford 1992; Cooper et al. 1999b). Research has consistently found that the divorced and separated have poorer health than the married, and single men but not single women report poorer health than their married counterparts (e.g., Verbrugge 1979; Morgan 1980; Anson 1989; Glaser and Grundy 1997).

Less sociological interest has been paid to health-risky behaviors in later life or how these relate to structural inequalities (Cooper et al. 1999a). Indeed, several UK surveys of health behavior in the early 1990s had an upper age limit of 74, suggesting an ageist assumption that health promotion was unimportant at this stage of the life course (Ginn et al. 1997). Among older people, marital status is likely to be linked to health behavior, especially for men. Married men may be advantaged because evidence shows that women have a primary role in maintaining a family "health watch," which may be increasingly salient in later life (Davidson and Arber 2004). Wives care for their husband's health in terms of acting as a "caretaker" to monitor their health behaviors and support positive health behavioral practices. Umbersen (1992) found that marital partners affected the health behavior of each other, with women more likely than men to have a positive influence on their partner's health behavior. Older men without a partner, therefore, lack many aspects of the supportive and health protective role of a wife. Thus, researchers might expect more damaging health practices among nonpartnered men. As discussed in the last section, nonpartnered men are also more likely to have reduced informal social networks because these too are most frequently generated and maintained by women throughout the life course (Scott and Wenger 1995).

Health and health behaviors are in part the product of events throughout the life course. Courtney (2000) argues that men take more health risks than women throughout their lives, which is primarily driven by the "machismo imperative" to compete and be seen as strong. Men's health in later life continues to be influenced by the social construction of appropriate masculine behavior (Kalache 2000). The threats to hegemonic masculinity associated with loss of a wife may lead to poorer mental health or engagement in health damaging behaviors. The current generation of older women have also been influenced by the socially constructed roles that shaped femininity throughout their life course—a generation for whom it was seen as less socially acceptable to smoke and drink. However, the likelihood of engaging in these health risk behaviors is also influenced by economic factors, social support networks, and social stress. An insufficient income may be a source of stress, leading to stress-reducing behaviors such as smoking and alcohol consumption (Cooper et al. 1999a). But on the other hand, a sufficient income is necessary for engagement in society—it determines the ability to socialize outside the home, which may itself link to alcohol consumption, as well as resources to purchase alcohol and cigarettes.

The next sections analyze how engagement in two health damaging behaviors—smoking and drinking alcohol above the recommended level—differs by gender and marital status, and to what extent these varying patterns can be explained by class, material circumstances, and social connectedness.

Smoking

A series of logistic regression models of current smoking is presented in Table 6.4. Model 1 analyses the eight-category gender/marital status interaction variable, while also controlling for five-year age groups. Both divorced men and women have much higher levels of smoking than other groups of older people, with odds ratios of 2.84 and 2.32 respectively compared to married men (OR = 1.0). Widowers also have elevated levels of smoking as do never married men, with ORs of 1.69 and 1.59 respectively. Married men and women are the least likely to smoke, followed by never married women. Smoking is therefore closely tied to partnership status in later life, with the divorced having high levels of smoking followed by widowers and never married men. This finding suggests that having a partner moderates adverse health behaviors, especially for men. The stresses associated with no longer having a partner, especially linked with being divorced, may lead to smoking.

Extensive research on working age groups has shown how smoking is linked to material disadvantage (Wardle et al. 1999). It was shown earlier that divorced and never married men have particularly disadvantaged material circumstances, as do divorced older women. All groups of nonpartnered women have poorer material resources, but the material disadvantage of never married women is less than for previously partnered women. Models 2–4 in Table 6.4 assess whether the higher levels of smoking of the divorced can be explained by their lower class, poorer material resources, and lack of social connectedness. These three sets of factors are shown in Figure 6.1, as potential explanations for the greater engagement in health risky behaviors of specific gender/marital status groups. Model 2 additionally includes occupational class based on last main occupation, as an indicator of their earlier life course. Model 3 includes material resources, namely household equivalized income, housing tenure, and car ownership. Finally, Model 4 includes measures of social connectedness.

As expected, there is an association of class with smoking, with higher odds ratios of smoking among the working class (skilled, OR = 1.42, and semi- and unskilled, OR = 1.53). However, comparing Models 1 and 2 shows that occupational class does not alter the odds ratios of smoking within gender/marital status groups. Thus, despite the known strong associations of smoking with social class, this does not explain the higher smoking levels of the divorced, because the odds ratios remain unchanged.

In contrast, the current material circumstances of older people have a very substantial influence on likelihood of smoking and explain a considerable proportion of the elevated smoking levels of divorced and never married men (see Model 3). Household equivalized income has a linear association with smoking, with older people in the lower 40 percent of the income distribution having an almost 70 percent higher odds of smoking than those in the highest quintile. Car ownership and home ownership are also measures of material well-being. Older people who do not own a car have an OR = 1.53 of smoking and renters have an OR = 1.50. These three indicators of

TABLE 6.4
Odds Ratios of Being a Current Smoker, Age 65+

	Model 1	Model 2	Model 3	Model 4
Age	+++	+++	+++	+++
65–69	1.00	1.00	1.00	1.00
70–74	.70**	.70**	.64**	.63**
75–79	.57**	.57**	.50**	.48**
80–84	.33**	.34**	.27**	.26**
85+	.17**	.17**	.14**	.12**
Gender – Marital Status	+++	+++	+++	+++
Men				
Married	1.00	1.00	1.00	1.00
Widowed	1.69**	1.63**	1.46*	1.56**
Divorced	2.84**	2.76**	2.04**	2.08**
Never Married	1.59**	1.55*	1.20	1.22
Women				
Married	.94	.94	.92	.94
Widowed	1.44**	1.40**	1.11**	1.15
Divorced	2.32**	2.32**	1.65*	1.78**
Never Married	1.19	1.25	.91	.96
Own Occupational Class		+++	Ns	Ns
I + II		1.00		
IIInm		1.08		
IIIm		1.42*		
IV + V		1.53**		
Household Income[a]			+++	+++
Highest Quintile			1.00	1.00
60–80%			1.40	1.41
40–60%			1.54*	1.53*
20–40%			1.69**	1.72**
Lowest Quintile			1.67**	1.68**
Car in Household			+++	+++
Yes			1.00	1.00
No			1.53**	1.46**
Housing Tenure			+++	+++
Owner Occupier			1.00	1.00
Renter			1.50**	1.50**

TABLE 6.4
(*continued*)

	Model 1	Model 2	Model 3	Model 4
Visiting Friend/Relatives				+ +
More than Once a Week				1.00
Once a Week Up to Monthly				1.29**
Less than Once a Month				1.47**
Chatting to Neighbours				+ +
Once a Week or More Often				1.00
Less than Once a Week				1.52**
Change in LLR	163.4	22.3	89.3	22.8
Change in df	11	3	6	3
N = 5,492.				
Null LLR = 4,730				

** Significance of difference from the reference category, * p < .05, ** p < .01

+ + Significance of variable in the model, + p < .05, + + p < .01, + + + p < .001

*a*Household income was equivalized for household composition using the McClements scale

Hosting friends/relatives was not statistically significant when included in Model 4

SOURCE: General Household Survey, 1994 and 1998 (author's analysis)

material well-being result in a reduction by about one-third in the odds ratio of smoking across each of the groups of nonpartnered older men and women; for example, the OR for divorced men falls from 2.76 to 2.04, and for never married men from 1.55 to 1.20. Occupational class is no longer statistically significant once these measures of current material resources are included in Model 3. These findings suggest that current material disadvantage contributes to the elevated smoking levels of nonpartnered older people, especially the divorced.

Regarding the three measures of social connectedness, *hosting* friends or relatives is not statistically significantly related to smoking (and was therefore omitted from Model 4). Those who *visit* friends or family more than weekly have the lowest levels of smoking (OR = 1.0), and those who visit less than monthly have the highest odds (OR = 1.47). Similarly, those who chat with neighbors less than weekly have higher odds of smoking (OR = 1.52). This suggests an effect of lack of social connectedness on smoking;

older people who have weaker relationships with family, friends, and neighbors are more likely to smoke. However, inclusion of the social connectedness variables in Model 4 does not alter the gender/marital status differences in smoking. In each case the odds ratios of smoking remain unchanged or *increase* once the social connectedness variables are included in the final model. Thus, the higher levels of smoking of divorced and widowed older people are not because of their lack of connections with friends, relatives, and neighbors.

Alcohol Consumption

Consumption of alcohol is more complex to analyze as a health risk behavior, because evidence shows that moderate drinking has beneficial health consequences, while excess alcohol consumption, especially binge drinking, has adverse health consequences (Hart et al. 1999; Wardle et al. 1999). Questions in the GHS asked about type and amounts of alcohol consumed, with responses combined into a measure of average number of units of alcohol consumed per week. One unit of alcohol is equivalent to a glass of wine, half a pint of beer, or one measure of spirits. This section examines drinking above the UK government recommended weekly amounts of 21 units for men and 14 units for women (Department of Health 1996), and also considers excessive drinking (above 50 units weekly for men and above 35 units for women), which is clearly hazardous to health (Cooper et al. 1999a). Overall, 20 percent of men age 65–74 and 12 percent over age 75 consume above the recommended level of 21 units per week, with only 4 percent and 2 percent respectively consuming over 50 units per week; see Table 6.5. Women's level of alcohol consumption is lower, 8 percent age 65–74 and 5 percent over age 75 consume above the recommended level of 14 units per week for women.

Married men and women are most likely to consume low or moderate amounts of alcohol, whereas nonpartnered women, widowers, and never married men are more likely to abstain or rarely drink (Table 6.5). For example, 67 percent of never married women never or rarely drink compared with 45 percent of married women. This finding suggests that being in a couple relationship promotes moderate drinking as a sociable activity. However, there is some evidence of polarization among never married men who are also more likely to be excessive drinkers—7 percent age 65–74 drinking above 50 units a week. Divorced men age 65–74 are the heaviest drinkers,

TABLE 6.5
Level of Weekly Alcohol Consumption[a]
by Marital Status, Gender, and Age Group

Alcohol Consumption[1]	Married	Widowed	Divorced	Never Married	Total
(a) Men					
Age 65–74					
Abstains	22	26	20	37	23
Low/Moderate	60	52	47	46	57
Above Recommended	15	18	22	10	16
Excessive	3	4	10	7	4
	100%	100%	100%	100%	100%
N=	(1,990)	(314)	(152)	(175)	(2,631)
Age 75+					
Abstains	33	32	32	43	33
Low/Moderate	56	54	52	42	55
Above Recommended	10	11	15	14	10
Excessive	2	2	0	2	2
	100%	100%	100%	100%	100%
N=	(1,004)	(490)	(40)	(65)	(1,599)
(b) Women					
Age 65–74					
Abstains	45	54	62	67	50
Low/Moderate	46	39	31	27	42
Above Recommended	8	6	6	5	7
Excessive	1	1	–	1	1
	100%	100%	100%	100%	100%
N=	(1,691)	(1,120)	(159)	(175)	(3,145)
Age 75+					
Abstains	55	61	55	66	59
Low/Moderate	39	35	39	30	36
Above Recommended	6	3	5	3	4
Excessive	1	1	1	1	1
	100%	100%	100%	100%	100%
N=	(645)	(1,551)	(84)	(187)	(2,467)

[a]Alcohol consumption: Abstains—Abstains or drinks under 1 unit of alcohol per week
Low/moderate—Under 22 units of alcohol per week for men, and under 15 units for women
Above recommended—22–50 units of alcohol per week for men, and 15–34 units for women
Excessive—Over 50 units of alcohol per week for men, and over 35 units for women

SOURCE: General Household Survey, 1994, 1996, and 1998 (author's analysis)

with a third consuming above the recommended level and 10 percent drinking above 50 units per week.

Consumption of alcohol above the recommended weekly limit (21 units for men and 14 units per week for women) is examined using logistic regression in Table 6.6. Model 1 shows a sharp gender division in the odds of consuming alcohol above the recommended level, with women in each marital status having an odds ratio of under half that of married men. Divorced older men are the most likely to drink above the recommended level (OR = 1.9) compared to married men (OR = 1.0). There is an elevated level for widowers (OR = 1.3), but never married men have equivalent odds to married men. The marital status pattern among women differs, with married women more likely to consume above the recommended level of alcohol (OR = .48) than previously partnered women. The lowest level of drinking is reported by never married older women (OR = .29).

It is important to recognize that *if* alcohol consumption above the recommended level is spread throughout the week (e.g., three glasses of wine per day for men and two glasses per day for women), this may in fact be health promoting, rather than health damaging (Hart et al. 1999). However, some older people consuming above the recommended levels consume very high quantities of alcohol either routinely or sporadically (as binge drinking) with serious health risks. The logistic regression analysis in Table 6.6 suggests divergent patterns, which may reflect this polarization in the beneficial and adverse consequences of alcohol consumption.

Unlike for smoking, occupational class has a *negative* association with high alcohol consumption. The highest classes (professional and managerial occupations) are most likely to consume above recommended alcohol levels (OR = 1.0) with half the odds ratio among older people previously in semi- and unskilled occupations (OR = 0.54); see Model 2. Financial resources have a strong and linear relationship to consuming high levels of alcohol, with the financially advantaged more likely to consume above the recommended levels. Older people in the lowest income quintile have an odds ratio of one-third of those in the highest quintile. Once income is included in Model 3, the association between class and high alcohol consumption moderates, but remains statistically significant. Neither car ownership nor housing tenure had a statistically significant effect on alcohol consumption, so were excluded from Model 3.

The link between marital status and consuming above the recommended

TABLE 6.6
Odds Ratios of Drinking Above the Recommended Level
(22 Units for Men and 14 Units for Women per Week), Age 65+

	Model 1	Model 2	Model 3
Age	+++	+++	+++
65–69	1.00	1.00	1.00
70–74	.80**	.80*	.86
75–79	.51**	.51**	.57**
80-84	.57**	.56**	.64**
85+	.23**	.22**	.26**
Gender—Marital Status	+++	+++	+++
Men			
Married	1.00	1.00	1.00
Widowed	1.31*	1.40**	1.35*
Divorced	1.90**	2.01**	2.18**
Never Married	1.03	1.10	1.15
Women			
Married	.48**	.53**	.54**
Widowed	.34**	.39**	.43**
Divorced	.36**	.39**	.46**
Never Married	.29**	.30**	.31**
Own Occupational Class		+++	+
I + II		1.00	1.00
IIInm		.73**	.83
IIIm		.74**	.99
IV+V		.54**	.74**
Household Income[a]			+++
Highest Quintile			1.00
60–80%			.75**
40–60%			.57**
20–40%			.47**
Lowest Quintile			.33**
Change in LLR	328.2	37.2	76.2
Change in df	11	3	4
N=8,202			
Null LLR=5,742			

** Significance of difference from the reference category, *p < .05, **p < .01

++Significance of variable in the model, +p < .05, ++p < .01, +++p < .001

[a]Household income was equivalised for household composition using the McClements scale.

Housing tenure and car ownership were not statistically significant when added to Model 3.

Social connectedness variables—frequency of hosting and visiting friends/relatives and chatting to neighbors were not statistically significant when added to Model 3 using 1994/1998 GHS data.

SOURCE: General Household Survey, 1994, 1996, and 1998 (author's analysis)

level of alcohol among men becomes *more* stark after including class and income in the models. The odds ratio for divorced men increases from 1.90 in Model 1 to 2.18 in Model 3. This finding shows that the elevated level of alcohol consumption among older divorced men is not explained by their poorer material resources, because disadvantaged material circumstances are linked to lower rather than higher alcohol consumption. The findings suggest that older divorced men are vulnerable to high levels of alcohol consumption, and that widowers also drink more than married men. However, in general more financially advantaged older people have higher levels of alcohol consumption, which may be consumed across the week with health promoting rather than health damaging effects. Married women have somewhat higher odds of above recommended levels of drinking than nonpartnered women, probably related to the social nature of moderate drinking with their husband.

It was surprising that none of the three indicators of social connectedness had a statistically significant effect on alcohol consumption when added to the final model containing occupational class and the material resource indicators.

DISCUSSION AND CONCLUSIONS

Analyses in this chapter lend support to theoretical ideas of *accumulation of advantage/disadvantage* in later life, extending previous research by illustrating that this process is linked to the marital biographies of older women and men but in gender-differentiated ways. Previous studies of later life have examined inequalities among older people based on class and current material resources, but few examine the intersection between gender and marital status.

The chapter has used large-scale British cross-sectional survey data to illustrate the distinctive marital trajectories and circumstances of groups of nonpartnered older people, who are often collapsed together in research using smaller samples. Although longitudinal studies are important for teasing out causal pathways, there is a lack of British studies of aging that are sufficiently large to reliably differentiate groups of nonpartnered older men and women. The chapter has illustrated how marital status is linked to material disadvantage, social connectedness, and two health behaviors in complex and gender-differentiated ways. Social connectedness with family, friends, and neighbors provides a source of companionship and sociability, a buffer against stress, and potential guardians of risky health behaviors. Inequalities in smoking in later life are not explained by class, but are linked to disadvantaged material circumstances, and the older person's marital status, particularly being divorced.

Marriage in later life for both men and women is associated with household material well-being, social connectedness, and lower levels of smoking. This advantaged state is the province of the majority of older men, because 70 percent of men over age 65 are married. However, for older women, being married is a minority experience, especially above age 75, when under a third are married.

Widowhood is the norm for women in later life. Although widows are materially disadvantaged compared to married women, they are similar to married women in their level of social contacts with relatives, friends, and neighbors. Widowers differ little from married men in their material circumstances and their social connectedness, apart from being less likely to *host* relatives or friends in their own home. Widowers are somewhat more likely to smoke and drink heavily than married older men, but this is not explained by their differential class, material resources, or social connectedness.

Divorced older men are particularly disadvantaged on all dimensions. They have a low social class and poor material circumstances; lack home-based social contacts with relatives, friends, and neighbors; and engage in more damaging health behaviors—showing the highest levels of smoking and alcohol consumption. Their high levels of smoking and drinking cannot be explained by their lack of social connectedness, but smoking is partially explained by their poorer material circumstances. Divorced older women are also materially disadvantaged, and have high levels of smoking, but unlike divorced men, they are equally integrated into social networks of relatives, friends, and neighbors as married women and widows. The proportion of divorced older people is projected to grow substantially over the next twenty years, reflecting cohort changes in UK divorce rates. It is particularly important to assess the policy implications of larger groups of divorced older men and women who may be very materially disadvantaged, exhibit higher levels of health risk behaviors, and of older divorced men who are socially isolated.

Never married older men are on average from a low social class and materially disadvantaged, but unlike divorced men do not have markedly elevated levels of smoking and drinking. Despite the fact that many never married older women were well-educated "career women," their income and car ownership levels are still lower than those of never married men, but they are less likely to engage in adverse health risk behaviors than any other group.

Among older women, the key divide in terms of material well-being is between materially advantaged partnered women and more disadvantaged nonpartnered women. Women who never married are better off in terms of class, income, housing, and car ownership than previously partnered women. This reflects differences in the process of gender relations across the life course, with never married women more likely to have had a longer occupational career and their own pension rights. Widowed and divorced women are materially disadvantaged in later life, having often spent much of their life subjugating their own occupational career to their roles as wife and mother. Older women are equally likely to be socially connected, irrespective of marital status. For older men the key divide is between married/widowed men who are materially and socially advantaged, and divorced/never married men who are not.

This chapter has shown that it is important to treat marital status as an analytic variable when analyzing inequality among women *and* men in later life. Drawing together what have usually been treated as separate fields of study, namely the analysis of class, material well-being, social connectedness, and health behaviors in later life has illuminated gendered patterns of advantage and disadvantage associated with marital relations across the life course. Married men and widowers are materially advantaged, socially advantaged, and have less risky health behaviors. In contrast, divorced men tend to be disadvantaged on all these dimensions, and are therefore more vulnerable in later life. Nonpartnered older women experience disadvantaged material circumstances compared to their married sisters, but older women are generally socially connected with relatives, friends, and neighbors, irrespective of their marital status. Divorced older women are particularly disadvantaged materially and have high levels of smoking.

Analyzing the intersection of gender and marital status in later life exemplifies the effects of gender relations across the life course; ever-partnered women's caring responsibilities have constrained their employment participation. Never married men have not benefited from the support provided by a partner for their employment career, but have had a lifetime to develop their own social activity patterns. Men who were previously partnered have lost the role of their wife in facilitating social networks and undertaking the health watch that supported their health promotive behavior. Thus, gendered relationships over the life course shape material well-being, social connectedness, and health behaviors in later life.

Hitherto, social stratification researchers have paid scant attention to the social patterning of inequality among older people, with the available research focused primarily on either class or gender. This chapter has advocated studying how the interaction between gender and marital status throws into sharp relief gender-differentiated processes associated with the life course that systematically pattern inequalities in later life.

Note

1. The analyses presented in this chapter were conducted as part of the ESRC-funded project on "Older Men: Their Social Worlds and Social Relationships," grant no. L480 25 4033. This work was conducted jointly with my colleagues Kate Davidson, Kim Perren, and Debora Price, and I am very grateful for their contribution to these analyses. I am grateful to the Office for National Statistics for permission to use data from the General Household Survey, and to the UK Data Archive and Manchester Computing Centre for access to the data.

References

Allan, G. 1985. *Family Life*. Oxford: Blackwell.

Anson, O. 1989. Marital Status and Women's Health Revisited: The Importance of a Proximate Adult. *Journal of Marriage and the Family* 51:185–194.

Arber, S. 1997. Comparing Inequalities in Women's and Men's Health: Britain in the 1990s. *Social Science and Medicine* 44(6): 773–787.

Arber, S. 2004. Gender, Marital Status, and Aging: Linking Material, Health and Social Resources. *Journal of Aging Studies* 18: 91–108.

Arber, S. and Evandrou, M. (eds.). 1993. *Ageing, Independence and the Life Course*. London: Jessica Kingsley.

Arber, S. and Ginn, J. 1991. *Gender and Later Life: A Sociological Analysis of Resources and Constraints*. London: Sage.

Arber, S. and Ginn, J. 1993. Gender and Inequalities in Health in Later Life. *Social Science and Medicine* 36(1): 33–46.

Arber, S. and Ginn, J. 2004. Ageing and Gender: Diversity and Change. *Social Trends 2004* 34, London: Office for National Statistics, The Stationery Office.

Arber, S., Price, D., Davidson, K., and Perren, K. 2003. Re-examining Gender and Marital Status: Material Well-being and Social Involvement. In *Gender and Ageing: Changing Roles and Relationships*, S. Arber, K. Davidson, and J. Ginn (eds.). Maidenhead: Open University Press.

Askham, J. 1994. Marriage Relationships of Older People. *Reviews of Clinical Gerontology* 4:261–268.

Bartley, M., Blane, D., and Davey Smith, G. (eds.). 1998. *The Sociology of Health Inequalities*. Oxford: Blackwell.

Bowling, A. 1995. The Most Important Things in Life. *International Journal of Health Sciences* 5(4): 169–175.

Bury, M. 1995. Ageing, Gender and Sociological Theory. In *Connecting Gender and Ageing: A Sociological Approach*, S. Arber and J. Ginn (eds.). Buckingham: Open University Press.

Calasanti, T. M and Slevin, K. F. 2001. *Gender, Social Inequalities, and Aging*. Walnut Creek, Calif.: AltaMira.

Cohen, S. 1988. Psychological Models of the Role of Social Support in the Etiology of Physical Disease. *Health Psychology* 7:269–297.

Cooper, H., Ginn, J., and Arber, S. 1999a. *Health-related Behaviour and Attitudes of Older People: A Secondary Analysis of National Datasets*. London: Health Education Authority.

Cooper, H., Arber, S., Fee, L., and Ginn, J. 1999b. *The Influence of Social Support and Social Capital on Health: A Review and Analysis of British Data*. London: Health Education Authority.

Courtney, W. H. 2000. Constructions of Masculinity and their Influence on Men's Well-being: A Theory of Gender and Health. *Social Science and Medicine* 50:1385–1401.

Davidson, K. 1999. Marriage in Retrospect: A Study of Older Widows and Widowers. In *With This Ring: Divorce, Intimacy and Cohabitation from a Multicultural Perspective*, R. Miller and S. Browning (eds.). Stamford, CT: JAI.

Davidson, K. 2000. What We Want: Older Widows and Widowers Speak for Themselves. *Practice* 12(1): 45–54.

Davidson, K. and Arber, S. 2004. Older Men: Their Health Behaviours and Partnership Status. In *Growing Older: Quality of Life in Old Age*, A. Walker and C. Hagan Hennessy (eds.). Maidenhead: Open University Press.

Davidson, K. Arber, S., and Ginn, J. 2000. The Gendered Meanings of Care Work within Late Life Marital Relationships. *Canadian Journal on Aging* 19(4): 536–53.

de Jong Gierveld, J. 2003. Social Networks and Social Well-being of Older Men and Women Living Alone. In *Gender and Ageing: Changing Roles and Relationships*, S. Arber, K. Davidson, and J. Ginn (eds.). Maidenhead: Open University Press.

Department of Health. 1996. *Health-Related Behaviour: An Epidemiological Overview*. Central Health Monitoring Unit. London: HMSO.

Department of Work and Pensions. 2002. *Households Below Average Income*. London: Department of Work and Pensions.

Farquhar, M. 1995. Elder People's Definitions of Quality of Life. *Social Science and Medicine* 41(10): 1439–1446.

Finch, J. and Mason, J. 1993. *Negotiating Family Responsibilities*. London: Routledge.

Fuhrer, R., Stansfeld, S., Chemali, J., and Shipley, M. J. 1999. Gender, Social Relations and Mental Health: Prospective Findings from an Occupational Cohort (Whitehall II Study). *Social Science and Medicine* 48:77–87.

Ginn, J. 2003. *Gender, Pensions and the Lifecourse*. Bristol: Policy Press.

Ginn, J. and Arber, S. 1999. Changing Patterns of Pension Inequality: The Shift from State to Private Sources. *Ageing and Society* 19:319–342.

Ginn, J., Arber, S., and Cooper, H. 1997. *Researching Older People's Health Needs and Health Promotion Issues*. London: Health Education Authority.

Ginn, J., Street, D., and Arber, S. (eds.). 2001. *Women, Work and Pensions: International Comparisons*. Buckingham: Open University Press.

Glaser, K. and Grundy, E. 1997. Marital Status and Long-term Illness in Great Britain. *Journal of Marriage and the Family* 59:156–164.

Goldthorpe, J. 1983. Women and Class Analysis: In Defence of the Conventional View. *Sociology* 17:465–488.

Hareven, T. K. and Adams, K. J. 1982. *Ageing and Life Course Transitions*. London: Tavistock.

Hart, C. L., Davey Smith, G., Hole, D. J., and Hawthorne, V. M. 1999. Alcohol Consumption and Mortality from All Causes, Coronary Heart Disease, and Stroke: Results from a Prospective Cohort Study of Scottish Men with 21 Years Follow Up. *British Medical Journal* 318:1725–1729.

Jerrome, D. 1996. Continuity and Change in the Study of Family Relationships. *Ageing and Society* 16(1): 91–104.

Kalache, A. 2000. Men, Ageing and Health. *The Aging Male* 3(1): 3–36.

Mackenbach, J. and Bakker, M. (eds.). 2002. *Reducing Inequalities in Health: A European Perspective*. London: Routledge.

McMullin, J. 1995. Theorizing Age and Gender Relations. In *Connecting Gender and Ageing: A Sociological Approach*, S. Arber and J. Ginn (eds.). Buckingham: Open University Press.

Morgan, M. 1980. Marital Status, Health, Illness and Service Use. *Social Science and Medicine* 14:633–643.

Norman, A. 1985. *Triple Jeopardy: Growing Old in a Second Homeland*. London: Centre for Policy on Ageing.

Office for National Statistics (ONS). 2003. *Population Trends 112*, London: The Stationery Office.

O'Rand, A. M. 1996. The Precious and the Precocious: Understanding Cumulative Disadvantage and Advantage over the Life Course. *The Gerontologist* 36(3): 230–238.

Pampel, F. 1998. *Aging, Social Inequality, and Public Policy*. Thousand Oaks, Calif.: Pine Forge.

Perren, K., Arber, S., and Davidson, K. 2003. Men's Organisational Affiliations in

Later Life: Influence of Social Class and Marital Status on Informal Group Membership. *Ageing and Society* 23(1): 69–82

Perren, K., Arber, S., and Davidson, K. 2004. Neighbouring in Later Life: The Influence of Socio-economic Resources, Gender and Household Composition on Neighbourly Relationships. *Sociology* 38(5): 959-978.

Phillipson, C. 1982. *Capitalism and the Construction of Old Age*. London: Macmillan.

Phillipson, C., Bernard, M., Phillips, J., and Ogg, J. 2001. *The Family and Community Life of Older People: Social Support and Social Networks in Three Urban Areas*. London: Routledge.

Price, D. and Ginn, J. 2003. Sharing the Crust? Gender, Partnership Status and Pension Poverty. In *Gender and Ageing: Changing Roles and Relationships*, S. Arber, K. Davidson, and J. Ginn (eds.). Maidenhead: Open University Press.

Scott, A. and Wenger, G. C. 1995. Gender and Social Support Networks in Later Life. In *Connecting Gender and Ageing: A Sociological Approach*, S. Arber and J. Ginn (eds.). Buckingham: Open University Press, 58–172.

Shaw, C. 1999. 1996-based Population Projections by Legal Marital Status for England and Wales. *Population Trends* 95:23–32.

Solomou, W., Richards, M., Huppert, F., Brayne, C., and Morgan, K. 1998. Divorce, Current Marital Status and Well-being in an Elderly Population. *International Journal of Law, Policy and the Family* 12:323–344.

Umbersen, D. 1992. Gender, Marital Status and the Social Control of Behaviour. *Social Science and Medicine* 34(8): 907–917.

Verbrugge, L. 1979. Marital Status and Health. *Journal of Marriage and the Family* 41:267–285.

Walker, A., Maher, J., Coulthard, M., Goddard, E., and Thomas, M. 2001. *Living in Britain: Results from the 2000/01 General Household Survey*. London: The Stationery Office.

Wardle, J., Farrell, M., Hillsdon, M., Jarvis, M., Sutton, S., and Thorogood, M. 1999. Smoking, Drinking, Physical Activity and Screening Uptake and Health Inequalities. In *Inequalities in Health: The Evidence*, D. Gordon, M. Shaw, D. Dorling, and Davey Smith, G. (eds.). Bristol: Policy Press.

Wenger, G. C., Davies, R., Shahtahmasebi, S., and Scott, A. 1996. Social Isolation and Loneliness in Old Age: Review and Model Refinement. *Ageing and Society* 16(3): 333–358.

Wyke, S. and Ford, G. 1992. Competing Explanations for Associations between Marital Status and Health. *Social Science and Medicine* 34(5): 525–532.

The authorized representative in the EU for product safety and compliance is:
Mare Nostrum Group
B.V Doelen 72
4831 GR Breda
The Netherlands

www.ingramcontent.com/pod-product-compliance
Lightning Source LLC
Chambersburg PA
CBHW020412290526
45785CB00002B/523